The Leap to Globalization

Creating New Value from Business Without Borders

Harry Korine

Pierre-Yves Gomez

Foreword by S. Ghoshal

JOSSEY-BASS
A Wiley Company
www.josseybass.com

658.049
K 84 L

Published by

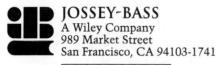

JOSSEY-BASS
A Wiley Company
989 Market Street
San Francisco, CA 94103-1741

www.josseybass.com

Jossey-Bass books and products are available through most bookstores. To contact Jossey-Bass directly, call (888) 378-2537, fax to (800) 605-2665, or visit our website at www.josseybass.com.

Substantial discounts on bulk quantities of Jossey-Bass books are available to corporations, professional associations, and other organizations. For details and discount information, contact the special sales department at Jossey-Bass.

We at Jossey-Bass strive to use the most environmentally sensitive paper stocks available to us. Our publications are printed on acid-free recycled stock whenever possible, and our paper always meets or exceeds minimum GPO and EPA requirements.

Jossey-Bass also publishes its books in a variety of electronic formats. Some content that appears in print may not be available in electronic books.

Library of Congress Cataloging-in-Publication Data

Korine, Harry, 1962–
The leap to globalization: creating new value from business without borders / by Harry Korine and Pierre-Yves Gomez; foreword by S. Ghoshal.—1st ed.
        p. cm.—(The Jossey-Bass business & management series)
    Includes bibliographical references and index.
    ISBN 0-7879-6211-2 (alk. paper)
    1. International business enterprises—Management.   I. Gomez,
Pierre-Yves.   II. Title.   III. Series.
HD62.4 .K668 2002
658'.049—dc21

2002000926

FIRST EDITION
HB Printing   10 9 8 7 6 5 4 3 2 1

The Jossey-Bass

Business & Management Series

Contents

Foreword

Professor Howard Stevensen, my teacher and mentor and a pioneer in making entrepreneurship a core area of research and teaching in business schools, once made the following point to me: "When I was 18 and had only $2,000 as my total resources and used that and as much money as I could borrow to buy an old, dilapidated house for $20,000 in order to restore it and then sell it at a profit, that was an entrepreneurial act. Now that I am 50 and worth a few million dollars, if I did exactly the same thing, would that be an entrepreneurial act?"

Entrepreneurship, as the question so vividly demonstrates, is relative. If one can comfortably spare all the resources one needs to pursue an opportunity that one can clearly see, it may still be good business to go after that opportunity but not much of a demonstration of entrepreneurship—unless that word is defined so broadly as to lose all meaning. This does not mean that entrepreneurship is the search for blind risk taking—indeed, as Howard was fond of saying, successful entrepreneurs do not wake up every morning asking what risks they can take that day; instead they ask what risks they can make their bankers take that day—but only that it requires a sense of will and a commitment to achieving something against odds that are formidable, given the entrepreneur's circumstances.

This, for me, is perhaps the most important point that Harry Korine and Pierre-Yves Gomez make in this book. *Globalization is an entrepreneurial process.* For a domestic company, whether large and established or small and a fledgling, the leap to globalization requires the vision, the will, and the daring that the 18-year-old Howard Stevensen demonstrated. Again the point is not that planning and prudence are unnecessary—indeed, as the authors show in this book, the risks of globalization need to and can be carefully managed—but that they are not substitutes for the total determination and absolute commitment of senior management to the leap.

Pierre-Yves and Harry provide numerous examples from their own research to substantiate this point. Let me add a few from my own limited experience. One of the companies I have studied in some depth is S.A. Chupa Chups, the world's largest producer of lollipops. Starting from a small sweetshop in Barcelona, Chupa Chups is today a truly global company, with operations spread across 130 countries. In terms of geographic origin, it is an exception. Spain is renowned for its sunny climate and sunny people, but not as a source of many global corporations. In terms of its business, lollipops are not an obvious core to build a global company around. At the heart of Chupa Chups's quite incredible success in globalization lies the entrepreneurial determination and courage of the company's founder and president, Enrique Bernat Fontlladosa. Of course, the company managed the global expansion process very well. Of course, it built the right organization, hired and developed the right people, shaped the right culture—all of that. But the wellspring for everything, at least in the initial phase of the leap of globalization, was the vision and the absolute, unwavering commitment of the founder and the small team he had built around him.

In sharp contrast, both Natura in Brazil and Bajaj Auto in India are highly admired companies, with records of outstanding success in their own home markets. Both have aspired to becoming global, and both have tried with, as yet, limited success. They had far better platforms for the leap compared to Chupa Chups—more resources, greater scale, better technology, perhaps more sophisticated leadership, too, in some ways. What they lacked is this determination, this commitment. They did not conceive globalization as an entrepreneurial process.

Once this essential point is understood, the rest of the arguments in this book follow quite naturally. Entrepreneurship implies novelty of some kind—a new combination of resources, in Schumpeter's terms—and the leap to globalization, therefore, needs a new value creation logic, based on a view of the overall global market. It was this view that allowed the then-small Chupa Chups to hire Salvadore Dali to design the globally standardized wrapper for its lollipops, and to invest in its own technology to develop machines capable of producing lollipops in volumes that were almost 100 times greater than the company's sales at that time. Enrique Bernat Fontlladosa visualized a standard product, produced in high scale with a global appeal, and built his entire business model on that vision.

Similarly, the authors' arguments about speed also follow quite naturally. The period when a company is going through the globalization process is essentially a highly unstable phase, between two relatively more stable phases—the domestic state, and the state of having become a global company. Momentum is essential for managing through unstable phases, as every bicycle rider knows. Like a top that can remain spinning only as long as energy is constantly supplied, a globalizing company can remain on its feet as long as it keeps moving, at a relatively high speed.

The need for unwavering commitment, a new business model, and speed, taken together, is a challenge that most business leaders would find quite unnerving. And that is precisely the value of this book. The leap to globalization is an enormously daunting task that is not for the fainthearted. But for those who have the ambition and the courage, this book will provide at least a rudimentary map of the very difficult terrain.

London, England   S. Ghoshal
March 2002

Acknowledgments

The research effort this book represents has substantially benefited from the support of many people and organizations. First, we would like to thank all the companies that cooperated in our study, and most particularly the executives and managers of our primary research sites, CMS Energy, Fresenius, and Gemplus. Their experience of making the leap to globalization has been the inspiration for this book.

Next, we owe a debt of gratitude to our home institutions, the London Business School and École de management de Lyon (EM Lyon). This book took early shape during the year Pierre-Yves Gomez spent at the London Business School as a visiting professor, and our work has benefited throughout from both schools' support for collaborative research. The Strategic Leadership Research Program at the London Business School and the Rodolphe Mérieux Foundation for Entrepreneurial Management at EM Lyon provided generous financial assistance.

A number of academic colleagues encouraged and critically advised our research effort. We especially wish to thank Sumantra Ghoshal and John Stopford of the London Business School and Roland Calori of EM Lyon for their unstinting support.

Our thanks also go to the hundreds of MBA students and executive education participants around the world who offered new inputs into our research process and helped us sharpen our thinking. Without the critical test of the classroom, we would not have been ready to commit our conclusions to paper.

Finally, a word of thanks to our editors, Susan Williams and Cedric Crocker of Jossey-Bass. Cedric's initial confidence in our material got this book under way and Susan's resolve in managing the revision significantly improved the final output. Our thanks to both for sticking with us over the lengthy process of making the idea of a book reality.

H. K.
P.-Y. G.

Introduction

Regardless of industry or size, today more and more companies face the globalization decision. With technological advances and market opening proceeding apace, and with globally oriented competitors taking aim at the last bastions of local dominance, globalization is at the top of the executive agenda. The subject of global strategy used to be the preserve of large multinational companies with decades of experience in operations abroad. Now even start-ups, let alone formerly local monopolies like telecommunications and utility companies, need to consider how business without borders affects them.

Over the last fifteen years, a great deal of scholarly work has gone into articulating the need for global strategies and describing their content. Among many others, Levitt (1983) on global products, Porter (1986, 1990) on global competition, and Prahalad and Doz (1987) as well as Bartlett and Ghoshal (1989) on the different types of global strategies have had a profound influence on how companies think about and conduct global business. Given the weight of the research and the wide dissemination of the findings, it is surprising that companies still consider globalization a major strategic and managerial challenge. From the definition of objectives to the implementation of actions, the process of globalizing is widely recognized to be a make-or-break growth stage for a company.

Why We Conducted Research on Globalization

The executives we meet in the course of our work as researchers and consultants all admit that globalization is an essential part of their competitive landscape. They do not, however, all have similar views on how to interpret the meaning of globalization for their industry or on how to succeed at globalizing. In spite of the considerable amount of knowledge available on the strategy of global companies, executives continue to consider globalization as a major challenge and are unsure of how to manage the process.

A great deal of the existing scholarly work on international business looks at how companies that already operate throughout the world can optimize their performance. In other words, this work investigates company practices once a global presence is *in place*. Research in this vein has extensively studied how companies such as Asea Brown Boveri (ABB), Procter & Gamble, and Ericsson coordinate their far-flung operations for competitive advantage. However, the process by which a company *transforms* a local or national presence into a global presence has not been studied in depth. Our research is directed toward understanding how companies have succeeded (or failed) at globalizing.

The origin of our research lies in the apparent gap between the weight of scholarly investigation and the evidence on the ground: although it may seem that everything has already been said and written about global strategies, executives standing on the verge of globalizing do not consider globalization to be a tightly structured, simple strategic problem. Instead they speak of globalization as one of their major challenges—an entrepreneurial venture into the future. A consensus that globalization is desirable seems to be developing among executives, but it is accompanied by significant uncertainty about the means of getting there. As we began to study the process of globalizing, it became apparent to us that globalizing companies had more in common than their objectives. Despite their considerable contextual differences, globalizers shared certain organizing patterns and management characteristics. This preliminary evidence that companies used similar means in globalizing encouraged us to inquire further whether success in globalizing could be traced to a set of general conditions.

As we explain in further detail in this Introduction and in the Appendix, we conducted field research on the process of globalizing in a broad variety of companies. Rather than analyzing strategic positions and organizational configurations resulting from globalization, we sought to document the entrepreneurial process employed in the transformation from local to global. Whereas previous research has concentrated on articulating *what* global strategies look like *once put in place*, we focus on *how* globalizing is realized *over time*. By comparing numerous cases from a variety of contexts, we hope to describe and explain what makes for a successful process of globalization.

Three basic observations have oriented our research. We have found that, first, globalization implies a redefinition of customer value and hence of strategy; second, that globalizing is an entrepreneurial process that transforms the company; and third, that speed plays an essential role in successful globalization.

Value Creation Reconsidered

First of all, it seems to us that the term *globalization* is generally used rather loosely in both researcher and executive parlance: when two professionals invoke globalization, they are not always talking about the same thing. A company becomes *international* when it exports the goods or services it produces beyond its home country borders. A company becomes *multinational* when it engages in production in multiple countries with a view to exploiting competitive advantage by integrating operations across borders. The processes of internationalization and multinationalization have been observed for many decades and are well understood.

What then are people really talking about when they say that a company is pursuing a global market? In the course of our research, we strongly sensed that executives draw a significant distinction between the terms *multinational* and *global*. A global market implies an integrated market and hence an original way of creating value for customers. Value comes not from exploiting differences across borders and locations but from capitalizing on the opportunity for business without borders. In a global market a company creates value by making its products, services, or competences available *anywhere*.

We believe that the current phase of globalization gripping so many markets cannot be understood without clearly distinguishing the value companies hope to create by globalizing. Globalizing is not equivalent to expanding geographically through the simple replication of existing business practices. It is based on a fundamentally different approach to value creation and hence on a redefinition of strategy. This approach is exemplified by companies like Amazon.com, which does not distinguish itself by providing books to customers but by providing a service that allows a student in Korea to order a book at the same time and under the same conditions as a student in Chicago; like WorldCom, which does not compete with established carriers for local business but offers clients like Ford Motor Company and Royal Dutch/Shell consistent communications anywhere around the world; and like Ispat, which is not renowned for its role as a leading steel specialist but for its ability to turn around ailing plants anywhere in the world, from Mexico to Germany.

Amazon.com, like WorldCom, Ispat, and most of the companies we studied, redefined how value is created in the industry. That redefinition was the necessary starting point for successful globalizing. Start-ups going global from the outset have brought with them a new way of creating value; established firms globalizing after years of domestic or multinational operations have made significant changes to their business model. Without an understanding of the way globalizing companies redefine the creation of value for their customers, we cannot do justice to our observations made in the field.

An Entrepreneurial Process

Our second basic research observation is that the globalization process is entrepreneurial. Companies that globalize successfully rely heavily on the ability of their leaders to engage key executives and management teams in a departure into an uncertain but promising future. Globalization cannot be accurately represented as a series of well-established steps to a predefined strategic and organizational end state. On the contrary, globalization appears to require great intellectual and emotional involvement from key women and men in the company so they can surmount unexpected external obstacles and overcome internal resistance to change. Whatever the strategic and resource context the company faces, an entrepreneurial process is always at work in globalizing.

Even for companies with decades of history behind them, globalization is a novel, entrepreneurial process that implies making radical choices and breaking with the past. For utilities and telecommunications companies established at the beginning of the twentieth century, for long-standing local champions in the dairy and retail banking sectors, and for the bookstore next door, everything is different. It should not be surprising, therefore, that globalizers tend to draw heavily on management practices commonly associated with new ventures: strong, entrepreneurial leadership from the top, broad-based sharing of strategy information, and decision making that goes against received wisdom. Not only does globalization imply a new way of creating value, it also poses questions about how to organize major change. In the globalizing processes we have observed, the management of the transition from nonglobal to global appears particularly important. However, even though the global firm has been the subject of considerable study, the management of the globalizing process has not yet received adequate research attention. Because we have found that successful globalization has much to do with the entrepreneurial abilities of leaders and managers, we have tried in this book to uncover how these abilities can be encouraged and channeled.

The Importance of Speed

Finally, we have observed that globalization today is accomplished by a *leap*. In what is perhaps the most dramatic aspect of the phenomenon, we have seen that companies globalize in a very short time, typically three to five years and in some sectors even less.

Consider these examples as initial evidence of the high speed that is characteristic of globalizing. Gemplus, the France-based smart card pioneer, built its very first factory with the capacity to supply ten times domestic demand and over five years established more than forty branches around the world—not just sales offices but also manufacturing plants and research and development sites; in 1993, CMS Energy was a local Michigan utility conducting minimal offshore oil and gas exploration—five years later, 35 percent of its assets were outside the United States, and it was conducting activities in twenty-six countries spread over five continents and all along the energy value chain; over the same five years, Fresenius (a medical care company founded in Germany in 1912) tripled the number of countries it served to forty and raised its percentage of non-German sales from 50 to 90 and its non-German personnel by a similar amount, in the process becoming the world leader in renal care. The globalization histories of Gemplus, CMS Energy, and Fresenius are not unique. In similarly short bursts of time, firms such as Cemex (cement), Ispat (steel), Parmalat (dairy), and SAP (e-business software and solutions) have also established a substantial network of foreign operations and taken positions of leadership in their industries worldwide. These examples are representative of the phenomenon that we call the *leap to globalization*.

Such leaps stand in marked contrast to the received wisdom on international expansion as expressed in the internationalization process literature, pioneered by Johanson and Vahlne (1977). Whereas this literature describes businesses taking a slow, culturally proximate approach based on gradually building up knowledge about doing business abroad, we have observed companies proceeding at great speed and with a broad geographical scope. The internationalization process literature treats expansion country by country; we have observed expansion against the backdrop of globalization.

We do not mean to imply that globalization requires acceleration or an increase in speed simply to be fashionable in this age when many things are being done faster. Rather, globalization requires speed because it is an all-or-nothing proposition: globalization occurs by a leap and not by small increments. High speed is a direct consequence. A leap can never be slow or proceed stepwise; a leap is a radical transformation and happens in one motion. Globalization by leap demands speed in the management of the process.

Our observation of high speed is consistent with our view of globalization as an entrepreneurial process. Entrepreneurial advantage is generally fleeting. Thus, unlike previous research that could largely neglect the temporal dimension of the globalization challenge, our study considers time a focal point for inquiry.

Our research has been framed by these three basic observations: successful globalization gives rise to a new opportunity for value creation, requires an entrepreneurial management process, and occurs by a leap. Our goal is to understand the economic conditions underlying and the management processes supporting the leap to globalization. How can companies successfully globalize at high speed? We believe that both executives and researchers can learn from a careful exploration of this question. Indeed, understanding the process of globalizing by leap may establish a new and stronger basis on which management can make global strategy prescriptions once a leap to globalization has occurred.

The Questions This Book Answers

Toward the end of their influential 1989 book on the emergence of the transnational corporation, Bartlett and Ghoshal noted that "despite their recognition of the environmental changes, each company (and many others we studied) stumbled as it attempted to implement its international strategic intentions" (p. 214). More than ten years later, we could make the same remark with regard to globalization but with a different emphasis. Once they have succeeded in becoming global, companies today do know how to put their strategic intentions into practice—there are a lot of tools available to help them do so. However, executives are finding that defining a global market and managing the entrepreneurial process underlying the leap to globalization is uncharted territory. Let us therefore address the questions executives are asking about globalization.

The first question we hear from executives may appear trivial, but answering it is essential for understanding the big picture: *what does globalization really mean in terms of creating value for the business?* As we said before, words like global and globalization can be and are put to multiple uses. However, a convincing strategy must be based on a clear view of added value. The efforts and sacrifices that globalization demands of an organization cannot be sustained if the strategy of globalization does not gain broad support in the company. Confusion about terms and slavery to fashion rarely make for strong commitment. To our thinking, and in the experience of many of the companies we studied, globalization implies a new way of creating value. Globalization is not a fad but a true strategic shift.

In Chapter One, we show that the current convergence of technological, political, and economic conditions allows companies to exploit a new source of strategic advantage. By globalizing, companies can go beyond *competitive advantage,* which is based on the ability to coordinate production and sales across national borders, to exploit what we call *compressive advantage.* Compressive advantage is based on the ability to market products, services, and competences anywhere, regardless of national borders.

The second question often asked by executives on the verge of globalization concerns risk: *how can the risks of globalization be evaluated?* Too often, globalization is presented as inevitable, a move that every company has to make. However, globalization entails significant risks: changing markets in order to exploit a new source of advantage means breaking with the past without being sure of the future. Experience shows that the executive's first challenge when anticipating a leap to globalization typically revolves around convincing his or her team of the need to act. Often executives feel that the key people around them do not really understand the economic changes the company faces or are simply resistant to change.

It seems to us that rigor and transparency offer the best means of persuasion. In our research the companies that clearly and openly worked through both the risks of not globalizing and the risks of globalizing were more likely to succeed in the leap to globalization. In Chapter Two, we provide an analytical tool for determining the risks a company faces if it does not globalize (namely, elimination from the market and exclusion from partnerships) and the risks entailed if it does decide to make the leap (namely, imitation and unsustainability). A comprehensive risk matrix allows the company to evaluate the trade-offs between these types of risks. The risk analysis tool we offer can help companies not only to understand their position in the globalization sweepstakes but also to visualize and discuss internal differences of opinion and make difficult choices.

A third question asked is, *how can the company manage the process of globalizing once the decision to leap has been made?* Again, the point of our research has not been to document best practice in companies that are already global but to understand what helps companies make a successful leap to globalization. Of course there are a large number of different management approaches, and it is illusory to imagine that a process as entrepreneurial as globalization can be completely captured in one best way. However, our research has tried to uncover the key recurring management practices in a successful process of globalization.

In Chapters Three, Four, and Five, we present the overall management framework induced from our research, in its three constituent parts: (1) *projection*—taking strategic action, as if industry globalization were already in place (Chapter Three); (2) *absorption*—creating specialized organizational competences that correspond to the risks of globalizing (Chapter Four); and (3) *harmonization*—timing structural and managerial changes in order to sustain the momentum of the leap to globalization (Chapter Five). Each part of this framework contributes in its own way to ensuring that the process of globalizing is managed effectively.

Chapter Six presents a synthesis of our framework. In the synthesis we insist on the interdependence of projection, absorption, and harmonization, and we elaborate on the management practices necessary for a successful leap to globalization.

Our seventh chapter, the Conclusion, addresses the question: *what is next for globalizers, what happens following the leap?* We argue that the most able globalizers have developed unique skills in managing the entrepreneurial process of globalizing and may be able to apply these skills in new contexts, leaping yet again.

The Empirical Basis of Our Findings

The findings reported in this book derive from four years of field research into the process of globalizing. In order to reduce the effects of size, industry, and country bias in our findings and to better reveal underlying patterns of successful globalization, we sought substantial variety in the sample of companies studied. The inquiry covered twenty-two companies from sixteen industrial sectors and nine home countries (for details of our research methodology and the names of the companies, see the Appendix).* All the companies in our sample had declared globalization to be a prime objective and had undertaken significant efforts to globalize in a short time. Some have come out on top of their industry races and are providing shareholders with superior returns; others have had to accept costly setbacks. In some cases, where the globalization game is still playing out, success and failure are not yet clearly distinguishable.

---

*From time to time in this book, we will refer to additional companies, over and above the twenty-two in our research sample. These examples are drawn from published sources and serve to supplement the text.

The research proceeded in two phases. In the first phase, we conducted in-depth case studies of the globalization histories of three companies with very different contexts: smart card pioneer Gemplus, a French start-up in a new industry; the utility CMS Energy, a purely domestic U.S. company in a deregulating industry; and renal care specialist Fresenius, a multinational German company in a nationally fragmented industry. The case studies drew on publicly available data, company archives, and multiple, extensive interviews with both senior executives and managers of operations in the field. We have maintained a research relationship with each of these three firms and periodically revisit to gather more data and update our information base.

In the second phase of our research, the preliminary conclusions drawn from the three first-phase case studies were tested and further refined in a larger but necessarily less detailed follow-up study of nineteen companies. For each of these nineteen companies, we oversaw the writing of a globalization history based on publicly available data and interviews with company executives.

This two-phase study allowed us to follow the globalizing process in detail and work out common points and differences among the companies studied. From the mass of data at our disposal, we induced the patterns of successful and unsuccessful globalizing processes. In the following chapters we summarize our research and propose a number of success factors emerging from our work.

We do not pretend to offer infallible recipes. As researchers, we have focused on explaining the phenomenon of globalization and on providing normative advice based on rigorous observation. We know that every company is unique and that the final responsibility for succeeding in the leap to globalization remains with company executives. Globalization is an entrepreneurial process, and no two entrepreneurial processes are exactly alike. However, we can suggest tools of analysis and management approaches based on best practice. This is what we have tried to do based on our research.

The Audience for This Book

We have written *The Leap to Globalization* primarily for executives in both established companies and start-ups. Yet we hope that this work also encourages academics to devote more attention to new topic areas in globalization. Global strategy and international management do not stop with the mature multinationals and established global strategies. This field of inquiry continues to generate new questions, and managers and students are not satisfied with easy answers. By focusing on growth over efficiency and transformation over optimization, research can open up new avenues toward understanding.

Chapter One

Understanding the Value in Globalization

All glass, metal, and modern functionality, with a giant atrium for large meetings, Fresenius's brand-new headquarters building contrasts markedly with the nearby historic spa town of Bad Homburg (close to Frankfurt) and stands as a monument to the remarkable transformation the company has recently gone through. In the seven years from 1992, when Gerd Krick took over as CEO, to 1999, Fresenius AG increased sales over sixfold to nearly DM 10 billion, earnings before interest and taxes (EBIT) thirteenfold, and employees fivefold. Particularly striking is the pace of international expansion: international sales have shot up from around 50 percent to 90 percent of the total, the percentage of Fresenius employees outside Germany has risen from 40 percent to 90 percent, and the number of countries in which Fresenius has operating subsidiaries has tripled from thirteen to forty.

In the early 1990s, Fresenius was merely one among many manufacturers of dialysis equipment. Like many other midsized companies with specialist expertise, Fresenius had patiently built on its reputation for high-quality products to establish an export presence in a few select foreign markets. Its principal offices were scattered in twelve buildings of varying functionality in and around Bad Homburg. Today the company is the world leader in renal care. From a narrow specialist niche in dialysis equipment, Fresenius has grown into a global one-stop shop for the treatment of renal disease, with a complete palette of equipment, clinics, and care plans on offer. In a few years, a company that traces its origins back to a fifteenth-century pharmacy has metamorphosed into an industry dynamo with global reach.

However dramatic, Fresenius's recent history is not an isolated example of the leap to globalization. On the contrary, more and more midsized niche players like Fresenius and also larger generalists previously limited to local markets are making a major move to embark on the adventure of business without borders and to play the global field. Fresenius's story finds echoes in the recent growth experiences of Italian dairy specialist Parmalat and Indian steel innovator Ispat as well as in the global expansion efforts of deregulated former monopolies like Deutsche Telekom or British Telecommunications (BT). Perhaps even more striking are the new age technology companies such as Yahoo! and Gemplus that were born with global ambitions in their business plans.

As we described earlier, a great deal has already been said and written about globalization—so much that almost every executive has to say he or she thinks about markets and organizations in global terms. Nonetheless, very little scholarly attention has been focused on the process whereby companies like Fresenius, Parmalat, Deutsche Telekom, and dozens of others are making dramatic leaps to globalization, adapting in a very short time to a market without borders. On what basis do executives make the decision to globalize their companies? What factors contribute to a successful leap to globalization? Finally, why does the leap to globalization typically entail a change in the company's business model and a very rapid growth process?

To answer these questions, we first explore the driving forces behind the decision to globalize. Too often, in our experience, executives believe globalization to be so obvious and necessary that they do not even ask why their companies should globalize. Yet the first lesson drawn from our research is that companies that succeed at globalizing always clearly and often systematically work out the rationale behind the move. At Fresenius, for example, Gerd Krick made several annual presentations to the board about globalization before he was named CEO and embarked upon globalizing the company. CMS Energy COO Vic Fryling worked closely with internationally experienced CMS board members from Ford and Upjohn to build support for his plans to initiate CMS global expansion. For strategists like Krick, Fryling, and others leading the companies in our sample, the decision to globalize was not a back-of-the-envelope solution to an emerging set of issues but the result of a detailed examination of competitive trends and company capabilities.

The question Why globalize? is indeed the essential point of departure in the process. The more precise the response, the greater the chance of making the leap successfully. If the need to globalize is not discussed and economically justified at the outset, then the entrepreneurial process required to bring the key people in the company onboard and to see the leap through will be undermined. Like any other major transformation in company strategy, globalization has to respond to two separate but equally important questions. First, in what way will globalization allow the company to create more value? Second, what changes in the business environment require the company to make a strategic decision on globalization? In the remainder of this chapter, we present a general guide for thinking about value and the business environment in the context of globalization. In determining whether or not to globalize, every company needs to formulate its own industry-specific response.

Value and the Meaning of Globalization

The international expansion of business is scarcely a recent phenomenon. People have sought to establish commerce beyond the frontiers of their own cities and states since the earliest days of historical record. The ancient Greeks had already established sites of production and exchange all around the Mediterranean in the sixth century B.C.; Indian merchants were traveling the Indian ocean from Africa to Malaysia in the first century A.D.; and the Portuguese had set up business outposts all over the world by the sixteenth century. The subsequent development of modern capitalism considerably accelerated the international expansion of business, and today exchange across borders is central to the well-being of every modern economy.

International expansion is old, but it is sometimes referred to with a new word: *globalization*. Why and when do companies, academics, commentators, and politicians choose to use globalization rather than *internationalization* or *multinationalization?* Is it merely a question of fashion? Can these and similar terms be used interchangeably to signify the same thing? In general usage these terms often are applied loosely, and such imprecise use has tended to obscure what distinguishes the current era from past eras from an economic historical perspective. Globalization does indeed have a specific meaning today, at the beginning of the twenty-first century, and executives must understand what globalization really means for their business before they can make strategic decisions about globalizing. Compared to past forms of international business expansion, globalization alters the economic rules of the game. In our research, companies making the leap to globalization all realized early in the process that globalization is not merely a question of *going international*. They understood and acted on the opportunity globalization presents to create new value for the customer and hence radically change the competitive landscape. What specifically, then, makes globalization different from internationalization and multinationalization? The difference lies in the way economic value is created under globalization. Consider this example.

The well-known courier company DHL currently has offices in 227 countries. In what sense can DHL be said to base its business on globalization? DHL creates value, a value the customer is willing to pay for, by making it possible for the customer to access and call on the company's services anywhere. Wherever the customer and wherever the customer's desired courier destination, DHL can deliver. The customer pays for DHL's services not because DHL is in a particular location but because DHL is capable of fulfilling the customer's need irrespective of location. The customer values a courier service that effectively takes the question of location out of the equation: with DHL, the customer knows for certain that location is irrelevant.

We would say DHL had an international business if the company were based in the United States and offered U.S. customers delivery of express mail and packages abroad. We would say DHL had a multinational business if the company offered its services at a better price by virtue of having offices around the world and exploiting economic advantages linked to its presence in the different countries (that is, by competing on cost). In fact, DHL is a *global business:* the company creates value for the customer by making location irrelevant. The customer is willing to pay the company in order to consistently obtain its service anywhere, anytime. The value the customer pays for arises from the irrelevance of location: the fact that he or she can get service from Bangkok to Paris as easily as from San Francisco to Buenos Aires is what gives the company's service value.

Global Offering = The Value for the Customer Arises
   from the Irrelevance of Location

Communication from and to anywhere is the very rationale of the Internet. Therefore it is not surprising that companies like Amazon.com or Yahoo! make globalization as we define the term a key platform in their business models. Amazon.com, as we noted earlier, is not a U.S. store that exports books, but a bookstore that is located anywhere and enables a student in Taiwan to order the same books at the same time as a student in Chicago. Amazon.com, like DHL, creates value by making location irrelevant to the customer. Looking only to the Internet, telecommunications, or courier services for examples of globalization, however, is to miss the forest for the trees.

Creating New Value Across Industries

Consider how Fresenius has used globalization to redefine the business of renal care. Until very recently, Fresenius, like other companies in its industry, saw itself as a provider of dialysis equipment to doctors and clinics. With a widely dispersed customer base and heavy governmental involvement both in offering care and regulating payment, this had been an eminently local business for a long time. However, in those countries (such as the United States) where health care was being privatized, larger chains of clinics and health maintenance organizations (HMOs) had begun to emerge. With its daring 1996 purchase of NMC, a U.S. company and the world's biggest dialysis clinic operator, Fresenius got a jump-start on the changes taking place in the industry. Fresenius could have continued to build relationships with local doctors in order to grow sales of its products in the traditional way. Instead, the firm transformed itself into the one-stop partner of choice in renal care, offering equipment, clinic operation, maintenance, and even patient risk management. Fresenius today provides value to HMOs, insurance companies, and governments around the world by ensuring a consistently high level of complete service no matter the location. Anywhere in the world where renal care is viable, Fresenius can be called upon to cover the needs of patients and payors, and it is this capability that gives the company a special edge.

Fresenius has globalized with a move from products to services. Ispat, a $3 billion steel company, has globalized by turning manufacturing into a transferable competence. Unlike its counterparts, the incumbent national steelmakers, Ispat's business is plant management know-how first and steel production second. First in Trinidad, then in Mexico, and more recently in Germany and the former Soviet Union, Indian Ispat takes on unwanted government steel plants and makes them profitable. Ispat's ability to find, buy, and turn around steel plants can be applied all over the world. In the process of doing business in many different countries, Ispat, like Fresenius, builds up local staff and expertise, but the essence of its success stems from providing a know-how–based service that is independent of location.

Even the best-known products and services can be rethought in order to create new value from the irrelevance of location. Thus, under the new direction of the innovative Ford Motor Company, the venerable Jaguar organization is contemplating selling not the car itself but the use of the car. Under this scheme the Jaguar owner would be able to pick up and drive a car of the exact same model in London, Paris, New York, Tokyo, and a host of other cities around the world. The new offering derives its value from usability—irrespective of location.

Among the successful globalizers in our research sample that were not start-ups, the leap to globalization entailed a redefinition of the value created and a change in the basic business model: thus, Fresenius transformed itself from a dialysis equipment manufacturer into a renal care company; WorldCom metamorphosed from offering long-distance voice telephony to offering data communications; and Cemex changed from old-fashioned cement maker to new age cement delivery logistics specialist. Successfully globalizing start-ups, such as Yahoo! or world smart card leader Gemplus, positioned themselves from the start to make location irrelevant to the customer.

At Gemplus, the business was defined not in terms of particular products or customers that might be location specific but in terms of smart card solutions *applicable in a wide variety of settings;* as a consequence the company makes and sells telephone cards in China, pay TV cards in Venezuela, and health care cards in the United States. Gemplus adds value by making its product-solution available anywhere. Of course, implementing the strategy of globalization does typically entail international expansion and country-specific investment. In the few years since its founding, Gemplus has become a complex organization with tentacles in dozens of countries. The tentacles serve the purpose of making the company's offerings available wherever the customer might require. The location and scale of card production is important to the cost side of the business equation, but the source of value to the customer is location independent. The offerings of Gemplus are credible and attractive to Venezuelan television, because the Venezuelan executive knows that Gemplus works well anywhere, whether the requirement be for telephone cards in China or for health care cards in the United States. The customer who buys from Gemplus or from Cisco Systems, for that matter, does not think of the purchase as French or U.S. high technology—it has been customized to his or her needs.

The customer does derive significant value from the fact that the products and services of these companies can and are being used by others anywhere.

Globalization can apply to products, services, or competences. Although globalization often entails a change of business model—from products to services as at Fresenius, for example, or from products to competences as at Ispat—such a change in and of itself is not equivalent to globalizing. A move into value-added services permits manufacturers to escape commoditization on the product side and capture more of the profits accruing to the product. Moreover, it aligns with the general decline of the production economy in the industrialized world. Services and competences become global, however, only when customers can, consistently, obtain them anywhere.

The products, services, or competences of a globalized company have added value because the location of provider and customer become irrelevant. Is consistent availability anywhere a key reason for customers to buy? Or, put another way, is the customer willing to pay for having access to the company's offering anywhere? If the answer is yes, globalization obtains. Table 1.1 illustrates our definition with some well-known examples. All the businesses cited in this table have international activities or serve customers from around the world but not all are global. The distinction we draw between global and nonglobal is critical to understanding how customer value is created.

Exploiting the Compressive Advantage

A new kind of customer value distinguishes globalization from all prior forms of international expansion: companies globalizing today understand that their customers will pay to do business irrespective of location. This first finding from our research has echoes in the sociology and economics literatures that have established globalization as a new and different form of economic expansion. The spirit

Table 1.1. Global and Nonglobal Products, Services, and Competences.

	Product	Service	Competence
Global	Coca-Cola (beverages)	Amazon.com (books and related goods)	Ispat (steel)
Value to customer	The value of Coca-Cola to the customer derives essentially from its availability in consistent form anywhere, with the assurance of equivalent quality and taste.	The value of Amazon.com's service lies in the provision of access to a vast collection of books and other products irrespective of the location of the customer.	Ispat's ability to turn around steel plants can be applied all over the world. It provides governments and institutions a know-how–based service that is independent of location.
International but nonglobal	Louis Vuitton (luxury goods)	W & G Foyle (books)	Mayo Clinic (medical care)
Value to customer	Although LV products are available in many stores around the world, the value of the products does not derive from this availability, but from the image and craftsmanship.	Although Foyle has been mailing books to clients around the world for over 200 years, the source of value is not access from anywhere but selection and tradition.	The services of the Mayo Clinic are available to fee-paying patients from anywhere, but it is the unique quality of treatment that patients value, not the availability.

of our definition of globalization recalls, for example, the *global village* that McLuhan and Fiore (1970) described in their seminal, early writing. Whereas the older forms of economic expansion—internationalization and multinationalization—apparently increase the size of the playing field (establishing more exchange and more sites of production), globalization seems on the contrary to reduce space (resulting in less diversity and smaller distances). Under globalization, value is created by compressing space and time to make location irrelevant. Or, to use Harvey's admirable expression (1989), we can say that *time-space compression* is the defining characteristic of globalization.

Comparing the different forms of international expansion, we note that the first wave of international expansion was characterized by international trade based on *comparative advantage*. As David Ricardo ([1817], 1992) documented in the early nineteenth century, comparative advantage is derived from differences in national productivity levels. Export and import are the outward manifestations of this form of the expansion of trade, and value for the customer arises from the trader's capacity to exploit productivity differences between countries that persist because of national borders.

A multinational economy is characterized by institutional arrangements, resource access patterns, and market definitions that differ from country to country and are governed by bilateral or multilateral country-to-country agreements. A firm operating in a multinational economy gains *competitive advantage* by adeptly managing the economic flows between countries or between sets of countries. Multinational companies thus characteristically organize production across multiple countries and optimize cost structures among the different sites. In this way they create value across borders.

Even though globalizing companies typically have some form of coherent, integrated management of operations worldwide, the integrated management of operations in the pursuit of competitive advantage does not by itself constitute globalization in our sense. In the case of globalization, national location per se is not an independent source of economic value. Instead, the source of value and growth lies in the capability to make an offering that customers can obtain irrespective of location. The firm gains a new form of economic advantage, one that we call a *compressive advantage*. By building a business without borders that seems to compress space and time, firms create new value for customers.

Becoming Global = Exploiting Compressive Advantage

Table 1.2 summarizes the basic differences among the three forms of international economic expansion.

From a historical perspective, we are at the entrance of a new era. From the seventeenth century onward, international business stood under the sign of mercantilism and was guided by the interests of the nation-state seeking to benefit from comparative advantage. Starting at the turn of the past century and reaching full bloom in the post–World War II period, multinational companies took center stage, exploiting competitive advantage across the world. With true globalization as envisioned by McLuhan and Fiore (1970) emerging at the end of the twentieth century, the ability to bring compressive advantage to bear and thereby to create new customer value becomes critical. The international, multinational, and global forms of economic expansion are of course not mutually exclusive—all three forms persist today (see Figure 1.1). Nevertheless, it is important to recognize that there are different forms of economic expansion and that globalization has unique characteristics and is not merely an extension of internationalization and multinationalization.

Table 1.2. Forms of International Economic Expansion.

Economic Form	Type of Advantage	Source of Growth	Organizing Principle
International	Comparative	Development of exchange among *nations*	Trade relations and resource levels *between countries*
Multinational	Competitive	Exploitation of national differences by *firms*	Internalized coordination *across borders*
Global	Compressive	Action on irrelevance of location for *customers*	Value creation from business *without borders*

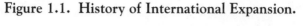

Figure 1.1. History of International Expansion.

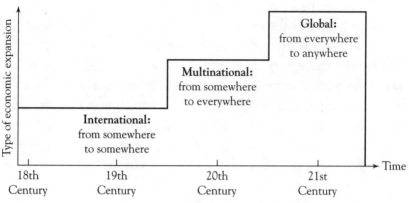

At the outset of this chapter, we said that it was essential for companies to ask, Why globalize? From the argument presented up to this point, it would certainly be wrong to conclude that all companies everywhere have no choice but to become global. We have shown only that globalization presents the opportunity for a company to create new value for the customer. Under what conditions does globalization become a strategic opportunity that needs to be acted upon? To address this second part of the Why globalize? question, we discuss how changes in the business environment shape the globalization decision.

Analyzing the Business Environment: Institutions, Resources, and Markets

Historians studying the evolution of economic systems over time define the business environment in terms of three principal dimensions: institutions, resources, and markets (compare Boyer, 1990). The coevolution of institutions, resources, and markets determines a company's business environment. By *institutions* (I), scholars mean the political bodies and legal frameworks that set rules of exchange and property rights. The term *resources* (R) designates the human competences, the technologies, and the financial assets available in the economy. The term *markets* (M), finally, encompasses competition and competitive interaction. An analysis of these three dimensions reveals what we call the *I-R-M structure* of an industry. An I-R-M structure analysis can be used both to describe the current economic context faced and to consider potential changes in the environment and the potential sources of value creation arising from such changes.

Today, in the world economic system as a whole, the institutions, resources, and markets that characterized the post–World War II era are in a heightened state of flux, with national borders becoming less relevant on all dimensions of the I-R-M structure.

Institutions. Nation-states are increasingly unable and unwilling to bear the costs of economic regulation and protectionism in support of national industries. With privatization, decreases in subsidies, and deregulation, national governments are less directly involved as economic actors. The gradual easing of governmental economic influence occurring in country after country has led to the removal of the weakest firms and the modification of existing industrial networks, putting considerable strain on existing competitive structures. As deregulation opens previously closed industries like utilities, telecommunications, health care, and even postal services to worldwide competition, the economic power of individual nation-states is further reduced, reinforcing the role adjustment already in progress.

Resources. Massive improvements in the speed, quality, and coverage of communications technology have made information sharing across borders much easier. As a result, it has become very hard today to create value only from national differences in information or know-how; for example, the viability of location-bound businesses such as bookstores is severely threatened by competitors that create value from the irrelevance of location. At the same time, the maturation of financial markets has severely reduced the importance of national location to financing. Financial resources are truly

global, on tap from anywhere, even for the start-up, and banks have
had to adapt their location-specific activities accordingly.

Markets. In many sectors, companies are actively driving cross-
border consolidation as well as cross-industry convergence. This action represents a change from the inside, an *endogenous perturbation*,
in markets, raising industry concentration and creating new, more
dangerous competitors. Over the course of the 1990s, both cross-
border and cross-industry merger and acquisition activity as well as
alliance formation exploded. Ten years ago, industry realignments
were far and few between and highly newsworthy. Today, people
hear that AT&T and NTT DoCoMo have signed a major partner-
ship agreement and know that it will be a big story for only twenty-
four hours—for tomorrow, Alcatel may be trying to take over
Lucent. With newly formed giants competing for position worldwide, the nature of competitive interaction in national markets is
fundamentally altered.

To the established business environment—with its strong national governments, preferential access to technology and capital,
and clearly delimited national industries—the cumulative weight
of these developments is staggering. The old, multinational economic system is breaking down, giving way to a new, global regime
in which borders and location are increasingly less relevant.

Given the reach and scale of these systemic changes, it is not
surprising that cases in which only one element of an industry's
I-R-M structure undergoes substantial modification are very rare in
our research. Telecommunications companies like WorldCom,
Telefonica, and Deutsche Telekom, for example, face massive regulatory change, technological upheaval, and market redefinition all
at the same time. Energy players like AES and CMS Energy are also
under pressure from all three sides of the I-R-M structure. Even Internet companies like Yahoo!, which might appear at first to be
moving only on the resources (technology) axis, face institutional
questions (for example, over content in a heretofore regulation-free
environment) and deal with the reality of practically continuous
challenges to the new market structure. Indeed, in most of the cases

we have studied, the entire business environment (the totality of the I-R-M structure) is in the process of major modification.

Fresenius CEO Krick, for example, based his company's leap to globalization on a carefully articulated analysis of the business environment. As early as 1990, he had reasoned that the impending privatization of health care (I) in many countries and the broad diffusion of basic dialysis technology (R) around the world would change the industry, implying a need for higher levels of concentration in equipment (M) and new business opportunities in health care (M). The now yellowed, original analysis paper is still tucked away in his office and reveals a compelling picture of how the industry would evolve from fifteen national and regional companies to three giant companies that span the globe and engage in multiple segments of the renal care value chain. This forward-looking I-R-M analysis precipitated Fresenius's successful leap to globalization.

Different companies face different I-R-M structures, and the rate of change of institutions, resources, and markets varies across industries. The process of globalization begins with a survey of the I-R-M structure of the business environment in which the company operates. The key question facing the company is this: will the foreseeable future bring changes to institutions, resources, and markets that would make it advantageous to exploit compressive advantage by offering a truly global product or service? The answer may be yes or no. Depending on the evolution of the company's I-R-M structure, globalization may or may not be the right objective. In any case, the reasons for globalization are rarely self-evident, and globalization failures can often be traced to inadequate I-R-M analysis. In contrast, successful globalizers take institutions, resources, and markets explicitly into account in their strategic reflection.

> Need to Become Global = Evolution of the Economic
> Environment Allows Exploitation of
> Compressive Advantage

It is important to keep in mind during the analysis that changes in the I-R-M structure of industries arise from both exogenous and endogenous sources. Thus changes in regulation derive from the interplay of government and business; an increased flow of techno-logical and financial resources is both cause and consequence of business development; and markets both shape and are shaped by company strategies.

If it is faced with significant environmental changes favoring globalization, a company can act in one of two ways: (1) resist the changes and maintain the strategic status quo, or (2) migrate out of the existing multinational system and transform itself to create new customer value from the irrelevance of location. For any company the choice of whether to resist or to transform depends on its posi-tion in the markets it serves, the perceived strength of the I-R-M modifications that favor the exploitation of compressive advantage, and its own capabilities for change.

As companies move to exploit the compressive advantage, they actually encourage the conditions that make the new, global I-R-M structure viable. Prompted by the systemic changes in their envi-ronment, much like would-be colonists by hunger, individual en-trepreneurial companies give up the old multinational world to set out for the expected El Dorado of globalization and attempt to ex-ploit compressive advantage. Each one's move to globalization fur-ther perturbs the multinational system and provides additional fuel for systemic change. Figure 1.2 depicts these forces at work.

In short, globalization is not a blanket expression for describing changes in the business environment nor should it be interpreted as fad or fashion. Globalization is deeply rooted in an evolution that affects the world economic system and gives rise to a specific new economic advantage, namely compressive advantage. This book de-scribes the entrepreneurial process through which companies can leap from the existing multinational state of the world to the emerg-ing global state.

Conclusion

In this first chapter we have made two essential points about the leap to globalization. First of all, we have stressed that globalization is based on a unique source of advantage. The compressive advan-

Figure 1.2. The Economic System in Flux.

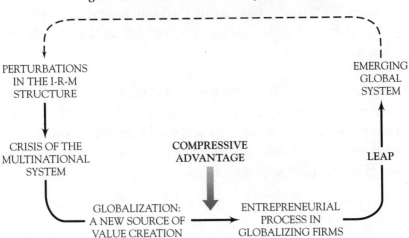

tage achieved through globalization implies a new and different way of creating value for the customer. If companies cannot create value by offering their products or services consistently anywhere, any-time or if customers will not pay for the irrelevance of location, then any attempt at globalization will fail.

Second, our research shows that globalization is neither fashion nor necessity. The leap to globalization takes place as a considered reaction to changes in the business environment—institutions, re-sources, and markets. The company and the entrepreneurs at its helm must have a clear view of this evolution in order to ensure that a strategy of globalization answers the call of a real business op-portunity. Mere ideas and enthusiasm are not sufficient. We stress that globalization is not a necessity for all companies in all situa-tions, and we offer two baseline questions for executives facing the globalization decision.

- Is significant modification of the industry's I-R-M structure foreseeable? The objective here is to take a precise reading of how regulatory, technological, and competitive developments are interacting to shape the company's future.

- Given any expected evolution of the I-R-M structure, are customers likely to ascribe particular value to products and services that are delivered in a consistent manner anywhere in the world?

However inviting the opportunity, globalization is fraught with risks that need to be evaluated before the decision to make the leap is taken. As a major strategic choice, globalization necessitates a careful review. With such a review in mind, the following chapter works through the risks of globalization.

Chapter Two

Facing the Risks of Globalization

In the previous chapter, we outlined the economic reasoning necessary to answer the question Why globalize? Globalization represents a major transformation in company strategy. Therefore the decision to globalize must be evaluated in terms of how the company can use globalization to create new value for customers and to respond to significant changes in its business environment. We showed that globalizing companies create value by making location irrelevant, exploiting the compressive advantage. We now move from the general argument to the specific case in order to inquire into the conditions under which a company should globalize. Or to put it more succinctly, when Starbucks chairman Howard Schultz says, "Starbucks is going to be a global brand, in the same genre as Coke or Disney" (Pendergrast, 2001, p. 47), how can one assess whether the company is making an appropriate strategic choice?

Although every company is affected to some degree by the larger systemic changes taking place today, the value creation opportunity and business environment differ across industries and technologies. In an effort to interpret and categorize the remarks made by executives of the companies in our research sample, we have developed a systematic method of analyzing the globalization decision. No company we studied has followed this method point by point. Instead, we have used our cases as the raw material out of which we have constructed a set of tests that can be used to work through the globalization decision. We discuss these tests in detail in this chapter and offer several examples of completed tests.

Two Types of Risk

As we described in the previous chapter, changes in the structure of institutions, resources, and markets can make globalization a potentially exciting opportunity for creating new value. The creation of new customer value, in turn, may help a company get a significant jump on the competition and stake out a good position on the emerging global playing field. However, opportunity goes hand in hand with risk. A new I-R-M structure implies new risks. If a company chooses not to globalize or at least not to globalize early, it may be left particularly vulnerable to the globalization of competitors. This line of reasoning introduces the first type of risk associated with globalization, namely the risks incurred by a company if it does not globalize. These risks are of primary concern in making the decision to globalize. If there is no economic risk in not globalizing, there is no reason for a company to go through the ambitious transformation globalization requires.

Conversely, if a company does globalize, it incurs risks associated with managing the transformation and the significant investment, rapid expansion, and increased rivalry that transformation entails. Globalization may look like a pot of gold at the end of the rainbow, but it is not easy to reach. A globalizing company may expend a great deal of effort yet ultimately fail to create new customer value. Given the real difficulty of managing globalization, it is important that the risks to be incurred be faced head on and not denied.

We stress the notion of risk because the companies we studied most closely were led by entrepreneurs who were highly risk conscious. Taken together, the top executives of Fresenius, CMS Energy, and Gemplus have a combined one hundred years of industry experience. From their various vantage points, Gerd Krick, Vic Fryling, and Marc Lassus have seen ups and downs, boom and bust. And yet not one of the three has ever moved as boldly in the past as he has in the last five years. Each one of these executives recognized and acted on a unique window of opportunity for his firm to globalize, in full recognition of the risks. Thus, when Gerd Krick envisioned the future of the renal care industry with only three major survivors, he was drawing the Fresenius board a graphic picture of the risks of not globalizing. CMS's Vic Fryling and his CFO Al Wright, during the company's globalization drive, put a great deal of emphasis on measuring financial and political risk, in the process developing best-of-class skills in these areas. Gemplus chairman Marc Lassus sold his house to fund the start-up, in full cognizance of the Boston Consulting Group report commissioned by his long-time employer, Thomson Microelectronics, that qualified the smart card business as "too risky," with "uncertain returns."

Major change appears always to pit opportunity against risk. Of course this dichotomy is not specific to globalization but pertains to every entrepreneurial context. The particularity of globalization lies in the desirability of leap change over incremental adaptation. It is necessary to leap because the strategic choice to be made does not center so much on opportunity and risk as on two different kinds of risks, the risks of not globalizing and the risks of globalizing in a competitive context. The final decision hinges on the entrepreneur's evaluation of these two types of risks and his or her propensity for action. In the following pages, we lay out a way to conduct a careful analysis of the risks associated with globalization and offer guidance on interpreting and acting on the analysis.

The Risks of Not Globalizing

Fundamental changes to institutions, resources, and markets alter the rules of the game and are the seedbed for globalization strategies based on compressive advantage. The evolution we describe plays out in a competitive context. As discussed in Chapter One, if one firm in an industry globalizes successfully, the pressure on others to globalize is reinforced. Once a generalized move to globalization gets under way, the initial decision to globalize can act like a self-fulfilling prophecy.

Change in an industry's I-R-M structure mixes the industry cards afresh. Globalization presents a unique opportunity to upset the industry hierarchy. In case after case in our research, we saw new or smaller players making use of the globalization opportunity to vault ahead of established competitors: WorldCom gets ahead of AT&T and BT in telecommunications; Fresenius gets ahead of Baxter International and Gambro in renal care; and Gemplus gets ahead of Groupe Bull and Schlumberger in smart cards.

The Risk of Elimination

With change in the I-R-M structure and globalization, an entire industry value chain becomes vulnerable to a redefinition of relationships. Because globalization offers new customer value, it reopens the battle for customers and market share. Both existing and new customers may be attracted to the anywhere, anytime value proposition, and competitors that do not globalize therefore stand to lose significant revenue and may eventually be absorbed by globalized rivals. The first risk of not globalizing then is on the demand side; we call it the *risk of elimination* from markets. The risk of elimination plays a principal role in contexts as seemingly far apart as Gerd Krick's survival scenario for Fresenius and WorldCom's inspired grab for new market share.

Globalization, by definition, leads a company to sell products, services, or competences that create value by rendering location irrelevant to the customer. From the outset of the process, then, a globalizing company conceives its expansion plans in terms of answering a demand that is not location specific and has the potential to be worldwide. The globalizing process consists of preempting as much of the new market as the company can before others come forward with comparable offerings and better value realization processes. In order to stave off the risk of elimination, globalizing companies make huge efforts to be first in the race to assemble the key organizational assets that allow them to provide seamless offerings anywhere: thus Fresenius *had* to get NMC before Baxter did; WorldCom beat out BT for MCI; and Spain-based Telefonica bid very high for the Internet network Lycos. What goes for buying assets to ensure market presence also holds for developing market footholds organically: utility globalizers like AES and CMS Energy find themselves bidding against each other in battle after battle for key market openings around the world; similarly, Yahoo! and America Online (AOL) race to open new locally adapted sites in country after country.

An assessment of the risk of elimination from not globalizing boils down to taking a view of both the evolution of the industry's I-R-M structure and the competitors' globalization strategies. The stronger the forces favoring globalization as a business opportunity to create new customer value, the higher the risk of elimination from not globalizing. As the cases of Fresenius and WorldCom, among others, show, globalization is commonly not the generally practiced way of creating value in an industry at the time the decision to make the leap is taken. Globalizing implies inventing the future, and assessing the risk of elimination is therefore not a trivial matter.

The Risk of Exclusion

Earlier we said that changes in the I-R-M structure accompanied by globalizing make it likely that relationships will be redefined throughout the entire industry value chain. The risk of elimination as a result of not globalizing pertains to the demand side of the value chain. On the supply side of the value chain, we identify a different risk—namely, the *risk of exclusion* from resource partnerships.

The risk of exclusion arises from differences in the degree of globalization across resource-interdependent industries. The globalizing firm typically is dependent upon globalized partners from other industries, requiring such resources as financing from global investors, components from global materials providers, and delivery of goods or services through global distributors. In the energy industry, for example, where long-term project financing is critical to viability, globalizing utilities have to develop the financial management skills to work successfully with global banks such as HSBC.

In industries such as energy and telecommunications that seek economies of scale in the purchase of equipment, globalizing companies strive to reach the size necessary to obtain reduced purchase prices from global providers like Siemens. Where standards are already established—as in computer programming, for example—globalizing companies have to work with the operating systems offered by Microsoft or Sun Microsystems.

Global companies generally prefer dealing with counterparts that are responsive to their global valuation and quality processes; this preference raises transaction costs for nonglobal firms. Nonglobal firms may have to pay considerably more for supplies and ultimately risk exclusion from critical resource networks. This risk of exclusion pressures firms to accelerate their own globalizing process in order to reach compatibility with partners before rivals do so.

The magnitude of the risk of exclusion as a result of not globalizing is a function of the globalizing firm's resource dependence: the higher the resource dependence on global partners, the greater the risk of exclusion. Often, smaller or more isolated firms have a clearer view of this risk than bigger players emerging from heretofore protected home markets. Internet security leader Check Point has its roots in Israel, and founder and CEO Gil Schwed says that Check Point's distance from lead markets "means we think about how to develop a product for somebody else, in the U.S. or globally" (Greenfield, 2001, p. 54). In contrast, companies like BT and the UK utility National Power have run into considerable difficulty with partners by insisting on exporting homegrown solutions. Assessing the risk of exclusion demands profound knowledge of the industry's supply structure. The company must be able to gauge the evolving requirements of banks, suppliers, and technology partners with some confidence before it can put a reliable estimate on its risk of exclusion.

Risks of *Not* Globalizing = Elimination from Markets
+ Exclusion from Partnerships

Assessing the Risks of Not Globalizing

Based on our research in twenty-two globalizing companies, we have established a test for assessing the risks of not globalizing. This test constitutes a heuristic with which to evaluate context-specific risks. That is, it is not a recipe but a thought tool: globalization is a gold rush, and in a gold rush there is no single recipe for success. The answer to the question of whether or not to globalize depends on the context under review. In our experience, a decision to globalize is too often treated as an article of faith. It should not be. This decision must be subjected to rigorous debate. Put simply, if one's customers do not value globalization (that is, do not benefit from the irrelevance of location) and one's partners do not require it, there is no reason to globalize, by leaping or otherwise. Conversely, if the failure to globalize means loss of key customers and weaker relationships with partners, then the risks of elimination and exclusion are high, and globalization may be the way forward. Thus the test in Figure 2.1 is meant to serve as a basis for globalization discussions at the executive level.

This test can and should be further customized to accommodate the characteristics of the I-R-M structure the company faces. For each question, thorough research is required. In our experience, increasing the number of questions does not add as much as going into depth on a few targeted questions. We also emphasize that executives should stick to tangible criteria and avoid sentiments in assessing the intensity of the risks.

If the risks of elimination from markets and exclusion from partnerships are high, RNG (the risk of not globalizing) is high, and consequently globalization is indicated. How high is high? The answer to this question is not straightforward. Clearly, the absolute value of RNG will always remain a subjective quantity, based as it is on a necessarily speculative assessment of customers', competitors', and partners' objectives. Moreover, there is no obvious cutoff point beyond which the risk of not globalizing is too high to resist.

Figure 2.1. The Risk of Not Globalizing (RNG).

	0 Low	1	2	3	4 High
Risk of elimination (from markets) 1a. How great is customer demand for a global offering? 1b. How committed are competitors to globalization? 1c. How important is a global offering to market share?					
1d. Mean risk of elimination: (1a + 1b + 1c) × (25/3) = ___ %					
Risk of exclusion (from resource partnerships) 2a. To what extent do lead partners require a global offering? 2b. To what extent do suppliers support a global offering? 2c. How much value do investors place on globalization?					
2d. Mean risk of exclusion: (2a + 2b + 2c) × (25/3) = ___ %					
RISK OF NOT GLOBALIZING: RNG = (1d + 2d) /2 = ___ %					

Ultimately, the test serves the purpose of focusing discussion, and the absolute values obtained should be understood as signals.

When we apply the test to the twenty-two companies in our research sample, at the time their decisions to globalize were taken, we find that their RNG values ranged from 55 percent to 85 percent. In general, companies in deregulating sectors such as utilities and telecommunications and also companies in high-tech sectors such as software faced the highest RNG values, between 75 percent and 85 percent. In these sectors, the risk of not globalizing is typically very high; thus executive debate centers instead on the risks of globalizing. In industries that are fragmented, with numerous small niche players occupying national and regional strongholds, the RNG value is usually lower, and the decision to globalize is a less obvious conclusion (see the sample calculation for Fresenius in Exhibit 2.1 starting on page 52). Companies in fragmented industries therefore often have a greater opportunity to surprise the competition, but the outcome is also less certain. In general, the higher the risk of not globalizing, the greater the pressure on a company to globalize by leap. Because both the risk of elimination and the risk of exclusion put a premium on speed, a high RNG value implies the need for a quick and decisive move to globalization.

The risk of not globalizing is often invoked by executives in explaining their strategic thinking to analysts and media: "everyone in the industry is expanding abroad like wildfire," or, "they are all going after the global customer." We wish to sound a note of caution here. As important as it is to make an honest assessment of the risk of not globalizing, a similarly realistic assessment of the risks of globalizing should always be an integral part of a company's globalization decision. Only by weighing both types of risk and by taking stock of their own propensity to act upon an uncertain future can executives do justice to the globalization challenge.

The Risks of Globalizing

In deciding to globalize, a company enters uncharted economic space. A globalizing company offers a new customer value proposition in an emerging economic space, but it is highly unlikely to remain alone in that space for long. Of the twenty-two companies in our research sample, not one—not even the most dominant companies in their respective sectors, such as Check Point and Bloomberg—have avoided rivals that offer essentially similar value propositions. Absent global regulatory institutions to replace diminishing national institutions, with few or no constraints on resource flows and disappearing market boundaries, the global economic space is extremely open, and companies entering it face two kinds of risk.

The Risk of Imitation

First, globalizing entails a high *risk of imitation*. The globalizing utility or telecom, for example, leaves its historically protected home

base and finds itself in direct competition with dozens of other formerly local monopolies, all trying to sell ostensibly similar services.
On the Internet, globalizers like Amazon.com find imitators taking
advantage of the open space at every turn in the road. The French
alapage.com and German buch.de are just two of them. Even in a
relatively obscure field of activity like steel plant turnaround, pioneer globalizer Ispat today faces a dozen rivals over each new business opportunity.

The value created from time-space compression typically revolves around skills and services that are difficult to patent and consequently do not form a legal barrier to entry. When more easily
patentable products or processes are involved, the general weakness
of property rights at the global level makes it difficult for a globalizing company to use the law to protect itself from imitation. The
choice of whether to globalize or not is therefore closely tied to the
nature of the know-how at a company's disposal and its ability to
put that know-how to use. To capture entrepreneurial profit from
globalization, just as from any other radical innovation strategy, a
company needs to base its value proposition on know-how that is
difficult to imitate. Because no know-how advantage can be of last-
ing duration, however, the globalizer needs to exploit its advantage
before imitators can act. Recently deregulated sectors with relatively small know-how differentials among companies are especially
vulnerable to imitation races. But even the globalization of the steel
plant turnaround business, an industry highly dependent on specialized know-how, illustrates the need for speed in coping with the
risk of imitation. In the mid-1990s, Ispat could confidently enter
negotiations for local or national steelmakers as the only credible
global player; today the company has to confront bidding situa-
tions with ten or more rivals vying for each steel plant turnaround
project.

The risk of imitation gives rise to a dilemma for companies that
would globalize. On the one hand, making the leap to globalization
gives companies a lead in the exploitation of compressive advantage; on the other hand, showing a new value proposition attracts
imitators. Because the exploitation of compressive advantage is not

protected by patents or by laws and because economies of scale and scope are necessarily small at the outset, the imitation dilemma of the first company to make the move toward globalization is particularly pronounced. The pioneer may ultimately find that it has invested substantial effort only to open the global space for its competitors, without having been able to capture a sizable proportion of the entrepreneurial profit. The more confident a firm can be about the specificity of its know-how and the quality of execution of its core processes, the lower the risk of imitation and the more advisable a move to globalization. In any case, the risk of imitation implies that if a company makes the move, it should leap: the best way to make imitation difficult for the competition is to jump very fast.

This discussion of the risk of imitation illustrates the kind of difficulties the globalization debate can raise in the boardroom. Should a company make the leap to globalization when the risks of not globalizing are high but company-specific know-how is limited and the risk of imitation is high? In our experience, the more clearly the risks both of not globalizing and of globalizing are drawn out in discussion, the more convincing the decision on globalization will be.

The Risk of Unsustainability

The risks of elimination, exclusion, and imitation all arise from changes in the I-R-M structure of industry. The same analysis of institutions, resources, and markets that points up the opportunity for globalization also reveals the risks inherent in the process and conditions the need to act. In addition to the two risks of not globalizing and the one risk of globalizing that follow from an I-R-M analysis, our research has identified a second risk of globalizing: the *risk of unsustainability*. This risk pertains to a company's ability to complete the leap to globalization and is a critical consideration in the decision to globalize.

In order to offer a truly global product, service, or competence and exploit the compressive advantage, a company typically needs to provide access points for its offerings worldwide. Worldwide expansion ensures the consistent quality of the anywhere, anytime value proposition. Where the risks of not globalizing are high and the risk of imitation is significant, the globalization process will turn into a race as companies move to capture the profits from compressive advantage ahead of their competitors. In the high-risk scenario that obtains for many deregulating industries, fragmented niche businesses, and high-technology activities, globalization becomes a double or quits game: a company cannot stop at the half-global mark. Once the globalization decision is taken, the globalizing effort has to be sustained. Because globalization requires significant human, financial, and technological investments, a company must generate sufficient payoffs en route to see the process through.

Risks of Globalizing = Imitation by Rivals + Unsustainability

Assessing the Risks of Globalizing

Parallel to the test for assessing the risks of not globalizing, we have set up a test for assessing the risks of imitation and unsustainability that arise from the globalizing process (Figure 2.2). This test too should be adapted to the company context. The critical issue is whether the company has the *capability* to globalize.

If the risk of globalizing (ROG) is high, globalization will be a particularly difficult management challenge. High ROG values indicate that a company will have to move very quickly to foreclose imitation and invest a great deal in its globalization process. The magnitude of the effort required and the likelihood of failure may convince top management that globalization comes at too high a price. A company must always weigh the risk of not globalizing against the risk of globalizing. If the RNG value indicates a strong need to globalize but the ROG value is daunting, executives may be justified in deciding to seek outside help rather than to pursue the globalization route on their own.

In our research sample, ROG values ranged from 70 percent to 95 percent (for examples, see Figures 2.3 and 2.4 and Exhibit 2.1). These relatively high values are explained by the fact that we did not

Figure 2.2. Test: The Risk of Globalizing (ROG).

	0 Low	1	2	3	4 High
Risk of imitation (by rivals) 3a. How vulnerable is a global offering to legal copying? 3b. How vulnerable are core processes to duplication? 3c. How negative is the impact of imitation on market share?					
3d. Mean risk of imitation: $(3a + 3b + 3c) \times (25/3) =$ ___ %					
Risk of unsustainability 4a. How great is the organizational effort required for globalizing? 4b. How great is the capital investment required for globalizing? 4c. How great would be the impact of a failure in globalization?					
4d. Mean risk of unsustainability: $(4a + 4b + 4c) \times (25/3) =$ ___ %					
RISK OF GLOBALIZING: ROG $= (3d + 4d) /2 =$ ___ %					

study any "easy" or market-dominant globalizers like Cisco Systems or Microsoft—cases in which the risks of imitation and unsustainability were and are still relatively low. Our sample was weighted toward cases in which globalization was a real management challenge. In the deregulating industries—utilities, telecommunications, and water—the lack of patents and the many relatively undifferentiated services offered imply a high risk of imitation, and the significant capital and organizational investments required for globalization imply a high risk of unsustainability. In fragmented industries with numerous specialist players, where products are prone to commoditization, the risk of imitation is also typically high, and the need to ramp up to global scale quickly implies a significant risk of unsustainability. In high-technology sectors, the nondominant players we studied, often start-ups, faced particularly high risks of globalizing. Interestingly, this also holds true for Internet pioneers like Amazon.com and Yahoo!

The very nature of the Internet makes imitation inevitable, and these companies have had to put significant effort into sustaining their globalization drive, each opening sites and offices in twenty or more countries in a very short time.

Applying the Tests

Calculations of RNG and ROG are not a matter of exact science. Our tests help companies find approximate readings for a particular point in time. The aim of the tests is to provide a basis for rigorous discussion about whether or not to make the leap to globalization. The questions may need to be adapted and refined to fit the particular business context under study, but the purpose of the tests is always the same: to clearly demonstrate both the risks of not globalizing and the risks of globalizing by bringing specific arguments to bear.

In our experience, working with the tests helps executives identify problems, share perspectives, and engage in converging opinions on the question of globalization. The tests can be administered at the outset of the leap to globalization or at any time that executives want to review their reasoning. The leap to globalization is an entrepreneurial process and must mobilize the energies of many people in the organization. The lone entrepreneur is likely to meet incomprehension and skepticism and may ultimately fail, perhaps blaming the failure on others' resistance to change or inertia. It is more useful to construct the globalization discussion around the notion of risks—resistance to change may be merely a matter of partial perception or imprecise debate. The *opportunity* of globalization may not be the best starting point for the entrepreneurial process. When executives build a globalization strategy around a shared understanding of the real *risks* to be incurred, they may come away with a stronger conviction of the appropriateness of their actions.

To illustrate the use of the globalization tests, we have applied them to the case of CMS Energy. (Tests for Fresenius and Gemplus are shown in Exhibit 2.1.) To recall, CMS Energy is a Michigan-based utility company with activities in all segments of the power and energy business. At the time it started its globalization drive, in 1993, the company faced impending deregulation both in the home market and abroad, significant technological development in power production, and marketing innovation all along the energy value chain (see Figure 2.3).

The analysis shows that CMS Energy's RNG is high. In an industry in which local governments are still very much involved and local monopolies are still common, is it justifiable to speak of globalization? Michigan customers like Ford or GM do have worldwide service requirements, but there is little evidence as yet to suggest that CMS (or its competitors) has made this kind of business a focus. Instead, national governments, particularly in developing countries, have been the key counterparts for globalization. In what sense do Argentina, Brazil, and India value anywhere, anytime, if at all?

Back in 1993, COO Vic Fryling put together a capability brochure demonstrating CMS's world-class capabilities, as evidence of his firm's credibility in the energy infrastructure world. Implicit in the claim that "we are the best" is the claim that "we can do it better than the competition anywhere." The track record of succeeding in developing country environments in Latin America, in turn, lends tangible support to the claim that CMS can bring its skills to bear in any such environment, be it India, Southeast Asia, or the Middle East. National governments value a strategy of anywhere, anytime as an assurance that they are dealing with the best and that the projects will succeed, no matter the local difficulties to be overcome.

Globalization was not always the objective at CMS. When he first visited Latin America in 1992–93, Vic Fryling was simply looking for international expansion opportunities. His thinking was local: "I talked to taxi drivers and housemaids to get a feeling for the people's commitment to deregulation and change." Very soon, however, Fryling recognized that the game was not only local. On CMS's first bids in Argentina, the competition came from all over the world: from Belgium (Tractebel) to Chile (Endesa). Wherever CMS

Figure 2.3. CMS Energy: Risk of Not Globalizing (1993).

	0 Low	1	2	3	4 High
Risk of elimination (from markets) 1a. *How great is customer demand for a global offering?* With deregulation, developing and developed countries want to be served by the world's best and to make bidding open. In addition, global customers like Ford may be looking to consolidate energy provision.				3	
1b. *How committed are competitors to globalization?* Rivals from around the world, some in the process of globalization, have begun competing on all opening markets and are also making first deals in CMS's U.S. home market.				3	
1c. *How important is a global offering to market share?* CMS Energy cannot grow further in its regulated Michigan market; if the company does not seek growth outside of Michigan, it becomes a sitting duck for non-Michigan and foreign predators.					4
1d. Mean risk of elimination: $(1a + 1b + 1c) \times (25/3) = 83\%$					
Risk of exclusion (from resource partnerships) 2a. *To what extent do lead partners require a global offering?* CMS meets the same industry and financial partners around the world, particularly global banks and engineering companies, with uniform procedure requirements.				3	
2b. *To what extent do suppliers support a global offering?* Key suppliers like Siemens and ABB give volume discounts of up to 30% on bundled purchases of major equipment and will offer preferred delivery dates to large customers.					4
2c. *How much value do investors place on globalization?* Investors value CMS primarily as a domestic utility and are not pushing for globalization.			2		
2d. Mean risk of exclusion: $(2a + 2b + 2c) \times (25/3) = 75\%$					
CMS'S RISK OF NOT GLOBALIZING: RNG = $(1d + 2d) / 2 = 79\%$					

went, the same governmental questions came up: who was CMS, and could the firm actually deliver on the country's energy infrastructure needs? Financing partners like Citibank employed the same processes in different countries and regions across the globe. Fryling saw that the world outside the United States was changing much faster than his home market and that he could prepare CMS for changes in the United States by gaining experience and establishing a position abroad. The limited protection CMS still enjoyed in the United States would "pay for globalization."

Of course not every firm in the large and growing energy infrastructure sweepstakes has interpreted the risks in the same way. The series of strategically unrelated deals put together by players like National Power and Tractebel look more like land grabs for foreign market space than globalization strategies. This is not to say that there is only one way to define globalization in energy infrastructure. CMS's regional integrator strategy for developing markets (regional integration anywhere, anytime) is different from Enron's trading and marketing emphasis and distinct from AES's independent power producer focus. The point is that not every firm racing to make energy deals around the world has made globalization an objective. CMS found its strategy "very early on" and has stuck by it, through ups and downs. In Vic Fryling's words, "CMS's objective is to become the foremost regional energy integrator."

An evaluation of CMS Energy's risk of globalizing is equally informative (Figure 2.4). Its ROG was slightly higher than its risk of not globalizing. Although Vic Fryling's capability brochure describes the company in glowing terms ("one of the best power companies in the world"), the reality was that at the time of CMS's globalization decision many other utilities possessed very similar skills in managing the energy value chain. As a result, many companies were able to overcome the capability hurdle set for market entry by liberalizing governments around the world, and the bidding for new projects was already highly competitive by 1993.

Moreover, the business and CMS's chosen strategy are highly capital intensive. This means there is strong pressure to perform

Figure 2.4. CMS Energy: Risk of Globalizing (1993).

	0 Low	1	2	3	4 High
Risk of imitation (by rivals)					
3a. *How vulnerable is a global offering to legal copying?* Energy infrastructure offerings are not copyrighted; moreover, CMS has not yet developed a unique value proposition. In a number of countries including Argentina, however, local monopolies are available.				3	
3b. *How vulnerable are core processes to duplication?* The core processes of identifying and implementing new business projects are common to all market players; as of 1993, CMS has not developed any special, difficult-to-imitate skills in these or other areas.				3	
3c. *How negative is the impact of imitation on market share?* In most cases, rivals compete for the same governmental contracts and concessions. Market share is directly dependent on proportion of bids won.					4
3d. Mean risk of imitation: (3a + 3b + 3c) × (25/3) = 92%					
Risk of unsustainability					
4a. *How significant is the organizational effort required for globalizing?* A smaller, specialized organizational unit is to be set up; the main body of the company will contribute engineering and operating expertise as needed. In addition, financial and political analysis skills need to be brought in-house.			2		
4b. *How significant is the capital investment required for globalizing?* A very significant proportion of new assets will be invested abroad (up to 50% planned by 2002). Major investment is required to gain a foothold in open-bid markets.					4
4c. *How great would be the impact of a failure in globalization?* Time and resources invested in globalization will not be available for development elsewhere, at a time when the business is also changing on technology and marketing dimensions.				3	
4d. Mean risk of unsustainability: (4a + 4b + 4c) × (25/3) = 75%					
RISK OF GLOBALIZING: ROG = (3d + 4c) /2 = 83%					

right away and little room for error or experimentation. If the globalization strategy is not well executed, the company will have significant debt and few alternatives to fall back on. In particular, in choosing globalization the company foregoes significant new business opportunities in marketing and trading—energy markets are changing so quickly that there is little time to recover lost ground.

Facing the Globalization Decision:
Entrepreneurial Attitude

As the case of CMS Energy illustrates, the risk of globalizing can be as high as the risk of not globalizing, if not higher. However, when the risk of not globalizing—over which the company has little or no control—is as high as in the case of CMS Energy, action on globalization is imperative. Indeed, although any cutoff point is necessarily artificial, our research experience is that a risk of not globalizing that exceeds 60 percent demands a response. Again, the risk of not globalizing is often the more obvious and encourages action, but if it decides to globalize, a company must develop an approach to minimizing the risks of globalizing. Success in the leap to globalization is dependent on how well a company can manage the tensions between the risks of not globalizing and the risks of globalizing.

In our experience, not paying proper attention to the risk of globalizing at the time of deciding to make the leap will have two negative consequences. First of all, the company will fail to prepare itself adequately to meet the risks of imitation and unsustainability. Second and perhaps just as important, if discussion of the risks of globalizing is only superficial, some members of the board and top management team may consider the effort a dangerous adventure and lend only half-hearted support.

CMS energy is not unusual in having risks of not globalizing and of globalizing that are practically equally high. In many of the cases we studied, the situation is similar. This finding underscores how difficult it is to make the globalization decision. Ultimately, that decision has to be an entrepreneurial choice. Where globalization is a double or quits proposition, the choice for or against the leap depends on the propensity for action of the top management and the organization. How courageous is the executive driving globalization? Does he or she have the legitimacy to mobilize the generals and the troops? The analysis also has to take the organizational context into account. What is the company's historical experience with large-bet strategies? Does company culture favor risk takers? If one maps *propensity for action* against the risk of not globalizing (as determined by the test) and also takes account of the risks of globalizing in the analysis, it is possible to get a fairly clear idea of how different companies will react to the globalization challenge (Figure 2.5).

Of course the two dimensions of the map may well be strongly correlated. For example, a weak propensity for action can explain why some executives and some companies do not anticipate the evolution of their business environment; conversely, an exaggerated propensity for action can lead a company toward immediate globalization when a more rigorous analysis of the situation might have shown globalization to be less urgent. These types of error can never

Figure 2.5. Attitude Map for the Leap to Globalization.

| | | Risk of Not Globalizing | |
		Low (<30%)	(>60%) High
Propensity for Action	High	EXPERIMENT The company starts into globalization to test its managerial capacities.	LEAP The company launches an entrepreneurial process based on clear strategic choices.
	Low	STAY PUT The company has neither need nor intention of considering a leap toward globalization.	LOOK FOR HELP The company knows that globalization is imperative, but is held back by the risks.

be avoided completely. Our aim in proposing tests and mapping risks and attitudes is to render the discussion of globalization as objective as possible and reduce the correlation between propensity for action and analysis.

Conclusion

We close Chapter Two by stressing that there is no inherent contradiction between an entrepreneurial attitude oriented toward action and an objective analysis of the business environment present and future.

> Decision to Globalize = Assessment of Risks
> + Entrepreneurial Attitude

It is important to distinguish between the risks of not globalizing (elimination, exclusion) and the risks of globalizing (imitation, unsustainability). Attention to the risks of elimination and exclusion primes the company for action; attention to the risks of imitation and unsustainability prevents the company from taking poorly advised action. Clarifying and discussing the risks associated with globalization will help executives distinguish among the strategic options available and, if the analysis so indicates, will help them mobilize the energy of the organization for the radical transformation that leaping to globalization entails. The following three chapters describe the strategic leadership, organizational competences, and management processes that our research shows contribute to a successful leap.

Exhibit 2.1. Globalization Tests
for Fresenius and Gemplus.

Risk of Not Globalizing: Fresenius, 1993.

	0 Low	1	2	3	4 High
Risk of elimination (from markets) 1a. *How great is customer demand for a global offering?* Health care to privatize; private payment to spread around the world.				3	
1b. *How committed are competitors to globalization?* Baxter and Gambro both appear to have global ambitions.				3	
1c. *How important is a global offering to market share?* Fresenius wants to be one of only three firms left standing.					4
1d. Mean risk of elimination: (1a + 1b + 1c) × (25/3) = 83%					
Risk of exclusion (from resource partnerships) 2a. *To what extent do lead partners require a global offering?* Potential new partnerships may be formed with globalizing insurers.			2		
2b. *To what extent do suppliers support a global offering?* Suppliers of materials are still national or regional in outlook.			2		
2c. *How much value do investors place on globalization?* House bank (Dresdner) and financial markets support expansion.				3	
2d. Mean risk of exclusion: (2a + 2b + 2c) × (25/3) = 58%					
RISK OF NOT GLOBALIZING: RNG = (1d + 2d) /2 = 71%					

Risk of Globalizing: Fresenius, 1993.

	0 Low	1	2	3	4 High
Risk of imitation (by rivals) 3a. *How vulnerable is a global offering to legal copying?* Many players offer essentially the same products and services.					4
3b. *How vulnerable are core processes to duplication?* Renal care clinics are run on the principle of replication; NMC is strong here.				3	
3c. *How negative is the impact of imitation on market share?* Although imitation is easy, the economic number of clinics per area is small.				3	
3d. Mean risk of imitation: $(3a + 3b + 3c) \times (25/3) = 83\%$					
Risk of unsustainability 4a. *How great is the organizational effort required for globalizing?* The organization has to shift from product to service, from Germany to U.S. base.					4
4b. *How great is the capital investment required for globalizing?* Capital expenditure for acquisitions is very high in the short term.					4
4c. *How great would be the impact of a failure in globalization?* The high debt ratio incurred would strangle the company in the event of failure.					4
4d. Mean risk of unsustainability: $(4a + 4b + 4c) \times (25/3) = 100\%$					
RISK OF GLOBALIZING: ROG $= (3d + 4d) /2 = 92\%$					

Commentary

At the time of this analysis (1993) the risk of not globalizing was considerably smaller than the risk of globalizing. In other words, Fresenius could have waited longer to globalize, but once the decision was taken, globalization had to occur by leap. The entrepreneurial personality of Gerd Krick determined that Fresenius would be an early mover. Krick's vision of privatized healthcare worldwide has not come to pass yet. However, and this is the crux of the story, the fact that Krick acted on his vision has forced competitors to act as well. Fresenius started a consolidation cycle based on a strategy of globalization well before regulations and customers had come around in ways that supported globalization. Once Fresenius had acted,

Gambro and other competitors faced altered globalization risks. The sheer size of Fresenius's engagements changed the nature of the game for all in the industry. In a business with limited opportunity for differentiation, the risk of imitation was already relatively high. Now, dialysis companies face clear threats of elimination, owing to the increasing numbers of health maintenance organization (HMO) customers who use a limited number of providers; of exclusion, owing to new service development partnerships with insurers; and of unsustainability, owing to the drive to ramp up for a global game in the making.

Risk of Not Globalizing: Gemplus, 1990.

	0 Low	1	2	3	4 High
Risk of elimination (from markets) 1a. *How great is customer demand for a global offering?* Smart card solutions can be applied anywhere.				3	
1b. *How committed are competitors to globalization?* Competitors Schlumberger and Bull are multinational, not global.			2		
1c. *How important is a global offering to market share?* Gemplus globalizes specifically to avoid domestic competition.					4
1d. Mean risk of elimination: (1a + 1b + 1c) × (25/3) = 75%					
Risk of exclusion (from resource partnerships) 2a. *To what extent do lead partners require a global offering?* Potential technology partners are globalizing software and hardware houses.				3	
2b. *To what extent do suppliers support a global offering?* Suppliers give volume discounts on component purchases.					4
2c. *How much value do investors place on globalization?* International investor group helps Gemplus enter new markets.				3	
2d. Mean risk of exclusion: (2a + 2b + 2c) × (25/3) = 83%					
RISK OF NOT GLOBALIZING: RNG = (1d + 2d) /2 = 79%					

Risk of Globalizing: Gemplus, 1990.

	0 Low	1	2	3	4 High
Risk of imitation (by rivals)					
3a. *How vulnerable is a global offering to legal copying?* Smart card technology is not exclusive to Gemplus.					4
3b. *How vulnerable are core processes to duplication?* Proprietary manufacturing and software advantages are set to erode.				3	
3c. *How negative is the impact of imitation on market share?* In many cases, imitators can compete for the same contracts.				3	
3d. Mean risk of imitation: $(3a + 3b + 3c) \times (25/3) = 83\%$					
Risk of unsustainability					
4a. *How great is the organizational effort required for globalizing?* Globalizing affects the whole value chain.					4
4b. *How great is the capital investment required for globalizing?* The minimum efficient plant size is very high relative to existing orders.					4
4c. *How great would be the impact of a failure in globalization?* As a start-up, the company has put a survival bet on globalization.					4
4d. Mean risk of unsustainability: $(4a + 4b + 4c) \times (25/3) = 100\%$					
RISK OF GLOBALIZING: ROG = $(3d + 4d) / 2 = 92\%$					

Commentary

Marc Lassus interpreted smart cards as ripe for globalization. Much as in the case of Gerd Frick at Fresenius, personal perspective was a prime determinant in the decision at Gemplus that a leap to globalization was necessary. At the time of this analysis (1990) a different manager with a different background would almost certainly have estimated the risk of not globalizing to be much lower. Lassus drew heavily on his past experience in related industries to evoke a high risk of elimination. The assessment presented here looks to the future: Schlumberger will be a global competitor; telecoms will deregulate further; microchips will become a part of everyday life. The risks of exclusion, imitation, and unsustainability are already very concrete, however. Smart cards were new in 1990, but in Lassus's view they formed part of a broader competitive ecosystem that was on its own trajectory toward globalization.

Chapter Three

Projection

Acting "As If" Global

"Executives in our company talk a lot about globalization without acting; . . . people tend to just ignore the talk." "Our actions contradict what the CEO is saying publicly; . . . we are really only putting derisory sums behind big strategic ambitions." "Serving the global customer is the declared objective, but the reality of what we are doing on the ground looks local to me." In the course of our research, we often heard such criticisms. In companies where globalization was presented as an imperative by top management, but actions did not follow words, employees had plenty of doubts. These doubts led us to inquire into the differences between vision and action in our research sample. Successful leaps to globalization, we found, are built on highly concrete actions.

Vision Versus Projection

Since the pioneering academic work of Joseph Schumpeter in the 1930s and Edith Penrose in the 1950s, the *visionary entrepreneur* is an integral part of any understanding of economic growth. The entrepreneur differs from other managers in that he or she has a unique *vision* of how the business environment will evolve and is prepared to act upon that vision. When it comes to globalization, we find that it is the entrepreneur's vision of the risks of both globalizing and not globalizing that gets the globalizing process started. But how is that vision transformed into action? How do the entrepreneurs at the heart of the globalizing process move beyond intentions and words? Our field research provides concrete evidence of the practices used by entrepreneurs to transform their visions of globalization into action. The term *projection* summarizes our findings: from the outset of the process, successful globalizers *project* themselves into the future and *act "as if"* globalization were already in place.

It is important to differentiate between acting as if globalization were already in place and merely having a vision of globalization. Managers with a vision of globalization will more often than not find themselves losing drive and direction in endless debates about the reality of the global village. The globalizing entrepreneur, in contrast, has *already* built a virtual house in the global village and is staking out large claims for more land. Acting as if globalization were already in place implies that the company implements the strategy, investment, and structure for anywhere, anytime value *today*. Whereas the majority of managers will move ahead only on a widely shared understanding of the present, the globalizing entrepreneur acts on a personal conception of the future. True to the Latin origins of the word *projection (proiectio)*, the entrepreneur throws *(iacit)* himself forward *(pro)*, acting as if the future were already reality.

For a clear example of projection, consider the situation in telecommunications just a few years ago in the mid-1990s. Around the world, regulatory barriers to foreign entry into national markets were falling, but not on all dimensions and not with equal speed; national incumbents, with their fully depreciated networks, could decisively counter foreign incursions; data communications clearly trailed voice in terms of customers' network use, both domestic and cross-border; multinational customers talked about wanting global providers but often acted differently in practice; and investors appeared wary of the telecommunications operators' international expansion efforts. Under these circumstances it was not at all clear that the market for telecommunications services would become global in the way it subsequently has.

Who would have been willing to take bets on globalization at that time? Most of the larger national telecommunications operators responded to the challenge of impending foreign competition by joining one of several alliance networks: Global One, Concert, Unisource, and so forth. Although different in many details, the three biggest alliances shared several key characteristics: (1) a focus on cross-border business, both voice and data, for multinational customers; (2) an agreement not to compete in the home countries of the alliance partners; and (3) different service offers in different markets, depending on the capabilities of the partner companies.

WorldCom took a different route, branching out decisively from its U.S. base in capacity reselling and regional operator consolidation. Between 1994 and 1996, the company made major acquisitions in international data service provision (WilTel Communications), international connection lines and agreements (IDB Systems), local access provision to U.S. cities and European financial centers (MFS Communications), and Internet service (UUNET). Thanks to these acquisitions and considerable further infrastructure buildup around the world, WorldCom put itself in a position to offer *all* fixed line telecom services around the world. The crowning acquisition of MCI in 1997 added a large customer base that could take advantage of WorldCom's unique service capability.

When WorldCom "stole" MCI from competing bidder BT, it was not just a win for the more attractive financial deal. Where BT wanted to acquire a U.S. operator to prepare for a future global telecom market, WorldCom had already put together a global scenario: the ability to offer all telecom services across its own networks to the global customers associated with MCI. Aided by a growing emphasis on data over voice, the globalization of customers, and the true liberalization of telecom markets around the world, WorldCom's strategy of global data services for businesses based on an Internet backbone and relying on owned end-to-end connections has become the industry model. Crippled by motivational differences and an inability to offer unified service to global customers, the old defensive alliances have been dissolved or are breaking up. Former national champions such as AT&T, BT, and Deutsche Telekom have been forced to reposition their international expansion efforts.

Was WorldCom simply lucky to favor data over voice and ownership over alliances in its drive toward globalization? Undoubtedly there is an element of luck in its story. The strategy evolved over time and responded to emerging opportunities like MFS and MCI. Nonetheless, there is a remarkable consistency to the WorldCom story. WorldCom's strategy of globalization turns out to be the one that the other telecommunications operators are emulating today, but it was questioned all along the way. The WorldCom model of end-to-end ownership, support of data over voice, and true global availability was ahead of its time. In spite of all the contemporary indications to the contrary, WorldCom put its money on globalization as if globalization were already common practice.

The practice of projection toward globalization is diametrically opposed to the traditional method of achieving international expansion. Although globalizers like WorldCom do learn along the way, the incremental accumulation of knowledge is not central to their strategies. Rather than evolving through well-defined stages of international activity, arranged according to increasing cultural distance and organizational complexity, companies making the globalizing transformation take their future context as given. They define their opportunity space and their international expansion trajectory by the anticipated future state of the world, not by the current state.

Viewed from the outside or even from an industry perspective, betting on globalization can look irrational. Ispat is a globalizer in steel, a highly protected industry in which export-based competition is strictly limited and globalization has long been a foreign word. Fresenius is a globalizer in renal care, an industry where the heavy hand of multiple national regulations might appear to rule out globalization for many years to come. But as governmental health experts debate the relative merits of different payment systems and local companies hope to hang on to niche markets, Fresenius CEO Gerd Krick has already established the kind of competitive position that makes his company a partner of choice worldwide, irrespective of the payment system. Recall that before Marc Lassus started Gemplus, his former employer had commissioned the Boston Consulting Group to study the smart card business opportunity. Drawing on research conducted in the U.S. market, where magnetic stripe cards dominated, BCG advised Thomson Microelectronics against smart cards. BCG's "no" set off a chain of events that put Marc in charge of his own future; within months he had launched the new company that was to take the smart card concept global.

When everyone says, "it can't be done; it won't happen in ten years," entrepreneurs like Lakshmi Mittal, founder and CEO of Ispat, Gerd Krick of Fresenius, Marc Lassus of Gemplus, and Bernie Ebbers, CEO of WorldCom not only see the opportunity but, more important, throw their companies into a world that does not yet exist. In so doing, they actively participate in the shaping of competitive conditions. When Bernie Ebbers says that "most of the [former governmental monopoly] companies in Europe would not be survivors [in open competition]," he is articulating the threat of a new world his actions have helped create.

Of course the logic of projection can and will lead to failure if the envisioned state of the world never comes into existence. Like the creation of a new company, the leap to globalization is an entrepreneurial process and is subject to a nontrivial rate of failure. The risk of failure cannot be separated from the process; it can only be controlled by appropriate management.

Unlike vision, projection revolves around concrete managerial action on the classical dimensions of market definition, investment, and leadership. What kinds of actions constitute projection toward globalization? What does it really mean to act as if globalization were already in place? Our research identified three executive actions as critical to projection: putting a strategy in place to *create new value* from globalization; aggressively *investing in the future today* to establish the basis for future dominance; and persuasively invoking globalization to *lead the charge* and rally the organization. Put together, these straightforward actions drive the globalizing company.

Creating New Value

As described in Chapter One, the leap to globalization is based on rethinking how the company creates value for customers. In the majority of the companies we have studied, the decisive rethinking of customer value takes place in the mind of one person, such as Gerd Krick at Fresenius; although in some others, such as Wal-Mart, a group of top managers or a coalition of managers across levels drives the process of questioning. In all cases, however, the future is the focus of attention, and all current assumptions about customers are fair game.

Through globalization a company has the potential to create new customer value and open up fresh market space. The critical variable to consider is the benefit that will be provided to the customer if a company makes access to its products, services, or competences seamlessly available from anywhere. Any reconfiguration of activities follows as a consequence of the company's pursuit of this compressive advantage. For example, Fresenius, says Krick, has set out to complete the value chain "from product, to hospital and care center management, to payment institution, and, finally, to patient." The point of departure for a strategy of globalization is the customer. What does the customer stand to gain from a global product or service? Will the customer pay for anywhere, anytime availability?

In asking these questions, a company needs to consider not only existing, well-known customers but also potential new customers likely to emerge as a result of future deregulation and technological development.

Existing Customers

Existing customers, whether corporations or individuals, not previously served anywhere, anytime may benefit in surprising ways and pay handsomely for the new value added.

Corporate Customers.   The existing corporate customers to be considered are those that have sites around the world and would like to standardize their suppliers and obtain a consistent level of service for the whole organization. This corporate customer target group for anywhere, anytime consists of companies like Ford and Shell that are themselves in the process of transitioning from multinational to global administration and operation. Until recently, these corporate giants managed services such as telecommunications, computer systems, and advertising and also value-adding activities like supply and distribution via a federation of loosely interdependent national units. To maximize sales to a Ford or a Shell, a supplier of products or services has had to match their national presence points one for one. As these companies centralize management support functions and respond to global competition by pulling dispersed activities together, they are also beginning to demand worldwide consistency and global solutions from their suppliers.

WorldCom understood this development sooner than the former national telecommunication monopolies and set out to build an infrastructure that would serve the emerging global needs of the transforming multinationals. Similarly, Bloomberg rode the wave of trading system standardization to provide clients like Merrill Lynch and Deutsche Bank global solutions and interconnected applications they could use from anywhere in the world. SAP expanded globally on the back of corporations' new need to build uniform enterprise resource planning systems. All these providers of anywhere, anytime value took business away from the erstwhile incumbents—national telecoms, country-based information services, and multinational system players—because their offerings were better aligned with the corporate customers' change trajectory. One way to create new value from globalization, then, is to get to the future before one's corporate customers and lend them a helping hand from the other side. Consequently, every company considering globalization needs to ask whether existing corporate customers can benefit from a truly global offering.

Individual Customers. The second kind of existing customer to value anywhere, anytime is the mobile individual: traveling executives, overseas students, tourists, and so forth. CNN was an early pioneer of a global service for the individual who travels the world and wants consistent service from anywhere. AOL, Amazon.com, Yahoo!, and even Jaguar, with its car on demand, are building market share on the same principle. The value to the user lies in the accessibility of the service; AOL is not present everywhere, but it is accessible in the same quality from anywhere. Consistent accessibility from anywhere is *the* selling point for the traveling executive who cannot rely on his local server (or news service) during business trips abroad but absolutely needs to stay connected.

Although Gemplus has grown primarily by serving globalizing telecoms, its own globalization can also be understood in terms of the mobile individual. From a global strategy point of view, smart cards are a key to unlocking new customer value from anywhere, anytime access. Gemplus founder Marc Lassus once described his conception of the smart card this way: "I dream of a guardian angel, an intimate personal object that accompanies its owner . . . that is a person's access key, memory, database, agenda, address book, wallet, and communication tool" (Marzloff & Glaziou, 1999, Foreword). Gemplus has not yet made individual mobility a focus of its marketing efforts, but the idea of portable *security solutions* has long been part of Lassus's approach and could be the basis for new growth in the future. According to Thian Yee Chua, managing director of Gemplus, Japan, Lassus "knew early on that the potential for smart cards was much broader than the early applications."

In assessing the market potential for the mobile customer, the key issue is the identification of a critical mass of potential customers whose mobility needs are currently inadequately addressed. If Gemplus, for example, were to make customer mobility a central focus of its strategy, it would need to find out who might value mobile security solutions and then determine whether the size of that potential market justifies the technological and commercial effort of devising and offering these solutions. Moreover, the solutions themselves could create new kinds of customer mobility.

New Customers

Existing customers are on everybody's radar screen already. All the telecoms want to serve accounts like Ford; every news media company has designs on mobile executives. What about new types of customers, customers that nobody is talking about yet? New customers such as globalizing companies and national governments may fundamentally alter the nature of competition, making the ability to work with them anywhere, anytime a necessary condition for corporate survival.

New Globalizing Customers. The question of value for customers needs to be looked at from a long-term perspective. Regulatory and technological changes in the business environment of potential corporate customers are likely to make national location increasingly irrelevant in these companies' business calculus. Fresenius's move from dialysis equipment into renal care, for example, jumps the gun on the privatization of health care and the advent of global health insurance and health management companies. Such companies do not really exist yet, but Fresenius has already maneuvered into position to serve them by assembling a global one-stop shop for renal care. If payment for health care is privatized in many countries, health maintenance organizations and insurance companies will also look to expand beyond their home bases, and they will find that Fresenius is able to service them with the entire complement of renal care offerings anywhere in the world.

Similarly, Enron's extension into water services preceded and perhaps helped hasten the development of trading markets for water that effectively do away with national borders. Deregulation typically leads to new rules of the game and attracts new players. Given the encompassing and systemic shift from multinational to global described in Chapter One, new rules and new players ultimately mean further opportunities for globalization, even in seemingly untouchable sectors like health care or water. The globalizing process anticipates these developments, and as we suggested in the cases of Fresenius and Enron, companies can, by their own projection, accelerate the advent of new global customers.

Technology may also set the stage for globalization. The Internet in particular is enabling anywhere, anytime service in a great variety of fields. By its very method of operation, the Internet reduces the relevance of location to customer value, giving customers the ability to search for the best solutions worldwide. This attracts many new service providers to the market and rewards companies that can actually deliver on the promise of anywhere, anytime to both corporations (as DoubleClick does) and individuals (as Amazon.com does). Again, technology on its own is only a trigger. The entrepreneur is the one who uses the technological development to redefine customer value and attract new globalizing customers.

New Government Customers. Paradoxically, even governments, which are among the most national and geographically fixed customers, may value the credibility the globalizing company offers. In the case of utilities like AES or CMS Energy, we see that national governments in the process of privatizing state assets value globalizing companies' reputation for technical competence and their demonstrated ability to carry out projects in a wide variety of locations. Ispat conveys a similar picture of excellence and the capacity to cope with national differences in steel. Thus, in connection with a recent and contested bid to take over the biggest steel plant in Romania, the company invited Romanian privatization officials to inspect its plant in Kazakhstan. Like the globalizing utilities, Ispat tries to convince national customers that the company has the capability to effect its magic anywhere—if it has worked in Kazakhstan, it will work in Romania.

Moreover, changes in the political environment and advances in technology can make even the most local of customers susceptible to a global offering. Around the globe, privatization of utilities and telecommunications companies has mandated openness and transparency, opening the field to globalizers that offer best-in-the-world service. Given more information and vastly improved communication technology, local customers can compare and contrast offerings from multiple providers. Traditional international business logic leaves these customers to the locally strong national firms and to the subsidiaries of multinational corporations. When local customers see value in anywhere, anytime service, they will flock to the globalizers.

Projection toward globalization is not equivalent to dreaming about the future of one's market, environment, and competitors. We find that the process of projection starts with a clear definition of existing and new customers and a forward-looking analysis of how customers might benefit from anywhere, anytime service, product, or competence. *Customers* come first. Customers—existing and new—are there to be won. Market, environment, and competition are then derived from the definition of customer value.

Investing in the Future Today

Every company talks about the future—very few companies act as if the future exists today. One of the critical distinctions of companies that make the leap to globalization is their record of action. Action means investment, putting money behind analysis and intuition. The way a company invests is a telling indicator of its commitment to the leap to globalization. The more closely current investment aligns with the eventual realization of a truly global market, the harder it is for a company to reverse course and stop short when doubts occur. Conversely, if investment stays cautious and limited, the company is unlikely to ever get off the ground. Through investment, a globalizing company seeks to achieve a preemptive fit with the entrepreneur's picture of the future state of the world. Anticipation of size, differentiation from the crowd, and ambition for world leadership—all carried out in the present—put the company in a position to cash in on the expected rush to globalization. The golden rule is to act as if one were already global.

Early Investment

Like parents purchasing clothes for growing children, today's globalizers buy several sizes too big, typically investing anywhere from two to four times as much yearly in new assets as do their industry counterparts without a global perspective. For example, with only a single order on the books (from France Telecom for one million cards) and few tangible leads for more business, Gemplus built its first factory with the capacity to produce ten million cards and immediately sought orders outside France. When Fresenius bought leading U.S. dialysis clinic operator NMC in 1996, it doubled its sales and personnel figures at a stroke. WorldCom has a long record of going in "too big." What is behind the early investment in a drive for size?

In many aspects of doing business, size lowers costs. When global sales are anticipated, achieving the size to yield scale economies in purchasing and manufacturing is often a primary objective. Coming into smart cards with thirty years of experience in semiconductors, with the "global perspective in his genes," Gemplus founder Marc Lassus naturally imported the scale calculus of chips and semiconductors. To Lassus, buying too big represented a calculated gamble that profitably sustaining the new business model required a manufacturing plant of a certain size. The same reasoning has been publicly mentioned by representatives of globalizers as diverse as Vodafone and Starbucks. The rush to globalization is often also a strategy of preemption. A company that reaches a cost-lowering size forces competitors to react; those that fear the risks of globalizing, namely the risk of unsustainability, will be scared off.

Just as important, putting size in place allows very rapid ramping up of production, in tune with the high growth rates expected if the company's new value proposition takes off. Because an anywhere, anytime strategy aims at a broad universe of customers, demand can explode. Clearly, companies like Fresenius are preparing themselves for just such an explosion. As in the cases of AOL, Yahoo!, and even WorldCom, when demand has taken off, the reputation resulting from being the first and the best to offer anywhere, anytime value can lead to a game of increasing returns, with the winner taking a large percentage of the business and becoming very hard to dislodge. Of course, significant early investment is not a guarantee of success but it is a prerequisite. Thus, although eToys.com spent three years and many millions of dollars building up powerful inventory management software, the company failed. Without the disproportionate early investment in sophisticated software, the company could never have realized its ambition of serving a global market in toys, but the software alone could not ensure the sales necessary to keep the company afloat. Again, we emphasize that globalization is an entrepreneurial process; a considerable risk of failure has always been part of the entrepreneurial game.

Differentiation from the Crowd

Early size is not the only defining characteristic of the successful globalizer's investment approach. Companies making the leap to globalization need to invest substantially in capital assets and human resources that do not match their current business environment or customer profile. In each case of projection we observed, investments in resources that enabled globalization served to differentiate the company from the competition and to prepare for demand.

Anywhere, anytime service is generally not the industry norm and achieving it requires substantial investment. Fresenius's preemptive investment in dialysis clinics *enabled* the company to completely redefine the dialysis value chain: through this investment action, Fresenius shifted marketing attention in the dialysis business from hospitals to care center management and insurers. Care center managers and insurers, in turn, would value the one-stop, worldwide renal care shopping that only Fresenius could provide. Not only did

Fresenius's bold move into clinics open brand-new business horizons, it also gave the company a significant *time lead* over its dialysis equipment competitors. A similar argument can be made for Cemex's early investments in worldwide logistics and shipping capabilities. These capabilities sharply reduced the relevance of plant location in cement production, making anywhere, anytime possible for Cemex and giving the company some competitive breathing space. Thus investment in capital assets at the start of the leap to globalization is useful when it serves to make the company substantially different, even if the difference cannot last very long.

Specialized human resources also serve a critical differentiating function. In practice, offering anywhere, anytime value is a difficult promise to keep, requiring leading human skills from very early on. Having the best specialists on your side—the top steel plant turnaround specialists as at Ispat—can provide a real edge. Commitment to a leap to globalization therefore also implies a race for talent in the specific skill segments a company needs if it is to create new value for customers.

Because the leap to globalization is based on a different way of understanding the business, companies need to look beyond the categories they are most familiar with: today, for example, Fresenius looks for doctors and actuaries more than for engineers. CMS Energy's pursuit of global leadership in regional power integration puts a premium on risk analysis over operating expertise. The human skills that fuel globalization today are generally service oriented and in short supply.

Ambition for World Leadership

Globalizers see the whole world as their opportunity space. To Gemplus's Marc Lassus, for example, the company's "battleground was not really France or even Europe. Because all our competitors were European, we had to go into territories where our competitors did not yet have their armies." Seeking out *high-potential* markets, Gemplus established sales offices in Singapore and the United States in the company's first year of existence. Rather than building international experience slowly and in culturally proximate markets, many pioneering companies undertaking the leap to globalization establish their first organizational beachheads in the key competitive arenas for global leadership. Both Yahoo! and DoubleClick set up their inaugural non-U.S. operations in Japan. Germany-based Fresenius launched its leap to globalization with a major push in the United States. Our research sample suggests that this kind of frontal attack appears to work best for companies that are first to become operational in a new customer value category and that can draw on a relatively large base market to start with. Such companies are most likely to clearly advertise their global ambitions from the start and then follow through.

Where base markets are small and cultural proximity can be a door opener, as in the Spanish drive to *recolonize* Latin America exemplified by Banco Santander (now BSCH) and Telefonica, first moves may initially be understood in the context of international expansion rather than globalization. Eventually, however, these first moves tend to be used as bargaining chips for establishing global competitive position. Telefonica's purchase of Lycos was funded from the success of the company's original Spanish-language Terra Networks. Banco Santander has tried to use its strong position in Latin America to muscle back in on Europe with a true anywhere, anytime offering.

Substantial investment serves the purpose of globalization because it makes globalizing talk credible, sending a clear signal to competitors, but also, just as important, to partner companies and employees. An investment that looks excessive to outsiders may actually be best likened to conquistador Francisco Pizarro's tactic of burning his ships: with their exit route cut off, Pizarro's men could not return to Spain and *had to* conquer America. Investing in the future today, as if globalization were already reality, is the best test of a company's convictions. Do executives believe in globalization enough to invest in productive resources that do not necessarily have present uses? Can they accept being labeled as overambitious or irrational? Are they able to explain why acting "as if" global is not crazy but rationally ambitious?

Leading the Charge

Once a company has succeeded at completing as dramatic a strategic transformation as the leap to globalization, observers have a natural tendency to admire the vision and courage of the entrepreneurs who made it happen. There is a tendency, however, to forget that success ultimately depends on the entrepreneur's ability to turn vision and courage into concrete and coherent organizational action. Because the very idea of a leap to globalization goes against received wisdom, building a shared perspective on the globalizing process is a challenging undertaking. We therefore sought to understand how executives transmitted the globalization imperative. Of course there are no simple recipes for executive leadership. However, in our research three elements stand out: the executive takes a stand in the company as the focal figure of the globalization effort, has deep knowledge of the industry, and communicates intensively with internal and external stakeholders.

Being a Focal Figure

Globalization appears to be strongly associated with personal leadership. Across the twenty-two cases we observed, successful leaps to globalization were invariably led from the top. At Italian dairy giant Parmalat, the globalization agenda is forever associated with the leadership of one man, CEO Carlo Tanzi. Over five years of extremely rapid expansion CMS Energy COO Vic Fryling acted as the company's Mr. Global, traveling six months of the year and negotiating with governments and key clients all over the world. Fresenius has its Gerd Krick; Gemplus its Marc Lassus; Cemex its CEO Lorenzo Zambrano.

Men like Tanzi and Fryling are both the architects and the public faces of their companies' leaps to globalization. Who are these executives, and what do they do? The leader of the globalization charge has deep knowledge of the industry, openly takes on the responsibility of being the focal figure in the globalization effort, and publicly articulates the company's conception of the future. The leader is the living symbol of projection toward globalization: he or she already stands in the new world and literally pulls the company and its partners forward.

In many larger companies, particularly in the deregulating telecommunications and energy sectors, globalization is paid lip service, but no single person stands for the cause. As a result, competing factions in the company prevent big moves, board members dissent, and skeptical investors harbor doubts about the company's intentions. If its CEO Ron Sommer had focused on globalization earlier, Deutsche Telekom might have targeted mobile services and the United States sooner; if Starbucks chairman Howard Schultz had articulated globalization as a primary objective early on rather than hesitating between a diversification focus and a globalization focus, the coffee chain could have moved more decisively in Europe, avoiding the late, expensive buyout of followers like the UK-based Seattle Coffee Company.

Contrast these situations of initial uncertainty with the state of affairs at Fresenius, where Gerd Krick unequivocally represents the globalization ambition of the company. "If you are truly convinced [überzeugt]," he explains, "you have to be willing to bet your career on it; if you aren't convinced, better do nothing. There is no in between." When questions arise at the operating level, people know what Krick would say and don't have to carry every decision to the top. When difficulties become apparent, as was the case with litigation concerns in the NMC purchase, both outsiders and insiders know who will take the heat. Because it is unprecedented and may appear irrational to observers, the leap to globalization needs such a focal figure in the company, one who makes a public commitment to carrying through the ambition and acts as a catalyst.

Having Deep Knowledge

Who are the focal figures for the leap to globalization? Are they the young, high-tech hotshots who grace the business magazine covers? We found that many if not all successful leaps to globalization in our study were undertaken by managers with significant industry experience—often twenty years or more. The particular combination of challenges associated with the leap—changing the business model, placing big bets, and galvanizing an organization and its stakeholders—appears to call for what Marc Lassus calls "geriatric teenagers" at the helm. The experience these leaders draw upon—their deep knowledge—consists of having managed through boom and bust, of having survived both success and failure.

The leap to globalization is both challenge and historic opportunity. A change of economic systems does not come along in every executive's lifetime. Whether sparked by deregulation, consolidating markets, or new technology, the leap to globalization represents a unique chance for senior managers to change the fundamental rules of the game. Deep knowledge of the industry appears to be a prerequisite for appreciating the magnitude of the shift taking place, and, more important, for having a strong sense of what it takes to come out on top in the new world.

From deep knowledge also stems conviction. Experience does not necessarily imply attachment to the status quo; on the contrary, what often makes the geriatric teenager the best person to lead the leap is the courage to act. People like Marc Lassus or Gerd Krick trust themselves. Their own track records of achievement in the industry give them the conviction needed to be bold. In many cases, they have just been waiting for the right opportunity to make their mark on the company and on the industry.

Engaging in Intensive Communication

The leap to globalization cannot be the work of one person alone, and the executive leadership of the globalizing process entails intensive, multilevel communication. Much like investment for globalization, communication for globalization revolves around projection: the executive communicates as if globalization were already in place. In a television interview following the company's dramatic move into clinics, Fresenius CEO Krick explains, "what was done by NMC in the U.S., we will do around the world; as funding for health care is privatized [outside the U.S.], you will have insurers taking care of payment." Krick speaks so confidently that audiences could come away with the impression that the global future of privately insured health care he describes is already fact. Yahoo! CEO Tim Koogle (in Geller, 2000, p. 14) talked of his search engine company as one of the "leaders in global branded networks"—a business that is still in swaddling clothes.

Communication oriented toward explaining changes in process gives people perspective on the actions of the company. Projection is primarily about actions that shape the future, but action without communication leaves much room for interpretation, inside and outside the company. Through the communications of leaders like Fryling, Krick, and Koogle, people know where the journey is taking them. This helps build solidarity among stakeholders. It can also give additional momentum to the very changes the executives are trying to achieve, by pulling competitors down the same path. Where pioneers like WorldCom go, experience shows that companies like AT&T and BT are likely to follow, albeit without the crucial first mover advantage.

Leading the process of globalizing and talking about globalization are not the same thing. The principle of acting as if global also applies to communication: to communicate as if globalization were already a fact. Thus it is not advisable to talk about how things will change in some distant future: such pronouncements often only disorient people. Globalization is best talked about in the present tense, with concrete actions to back up the discourse. Concrete actions are the true measure of the leader's commitment to globalizing.

Conclusion

What does it take for a company to project toward globalization? This chapter has provided a blueprint for action: come up with ways to create new value for customers, invest in the future today, and lead the charge with a sense of history and commitment. Taken one by one, these actions are a part of every executive's toolkit and do not promise much that is new or different; employed in combination, however, they constitute a powerful force for change.

Projection = Creating New Value + Early Investment
+ Leading the Charge

Projection is an entrepreneurial act that influences the whole company. Acting as if the company were global propels it toward globalization. It is important to keep in mind that projection is not only or even primarily about thinking up new ways of creating value: projection implies *acting upon* opportunity with an entrepreneur's unique sense of time—well in advance of the point when a business idea becomes common knowledge or accepted wisdom. Clearly this kind of action will not happen if management seeks to avoid uncertainty at all costs. The leap to globalization is always an attempt to take on uncertainty by actively shaping the future.

Three questions can be asked to test whether a company is engaging in projection:

1. Do executives talk concretely about actions for globalization (rather than abstractly about a need for globalization)?

2. Have tangible, substantial actions been undertaken

   - To serve global clients?
   - To differentiate global investments?
   - To prove global leadership?

3. Is the globalization process *incarnated* in a legitimate leader?

A globalizing company should be able answer all these questions positively. In our experience, organizational failure in projecting toward globalization occurs for these reasons:

- The company's effort is found wanting in one or several of the ways our questions point to.
- There is a disconnect between vision and action.

To this point we have frequently emphasized the important role played by top management, often the chief executive in person. We do not consider top management to be all powerful, and Chapters Four and Five are devoted to discussing the organizational competences and management processes behind a successful leap to globalization. Nonetheless there should be no doubt that the thinking, investing, and leading that bring projection into being require strong guidance from the top.

Chapter Four

Absorption

Tackling the Risks of Globalizing

No single executive alone can accomplish the entrepreneurial transformation globalization requires. Projection is but one part of the leap to globalization. Likewise having the right idea and making the right investment at the right time are merely necessary conditions. The executive actions described in the previous chapter make sense only in the context of a broader organizational push. The leap will not succeed without the right organizational competences and supporting processes. The business has to maintain strong momentum, digest substantial growth, and be ready to change course in midflight if necessary. What stresses and adjustments are required to perform to these specifications?

As we outlined in the Introduction and have emphasized throughout this book, our research focuses on the *process* of globalizing, the transition from nonglobal to global. Therefore we directed our inquiry toward building an understanding of the executive and organizational effort it takes to support the transition. Contrary to our initial expectations, we found that the majority of globalizing companies we studied did not fundamentally alter their organizational structures during the leap. Most outwardly visible structural adjustments took the form of new international finance and legal departments or regional administration divisions. Only a handful of our sample companies adopted the global organization characteristics described by Prahalad and Doz (1987) and Bartlett and Ghoshal (1989).

If not by a major structural transformation, how else do globalizers support a leap in growth? Our research identified a powerful process for coping with this challenge. Rather than denying the risks of globalization or trying to protect itself against them, the successful globalizer tackles the risks head on. So pervasive was this process in our data that we applied the term *absorption* to it. Rather than restructuring along geographical or product lines to cope with the changes in its business, the globalizing company reorients its organization around the process of absorbing risks.

Growing by Absorbing Risks

Risk absorption takes on great importance in managing the process of globalizing because the economic risks of globalizing are what spur the leap in the first place. Country differences and coordination between countries—the traditional management challenges of the multinational company—are of secondary importance to the globalizer. First and foremost, the globalizer is concerned with the risks and the corresponding implications for growth that we described in Chapter Two:

1. *Risk of elimination from markets:* occupy as much of the new market as you can *before* competitors take your place with better value realization processes.

2. *Risk of exclusion from resource partnerships:* accelerate the globalizing process so as to reach compatibility with partners *before* your rivals do.

3. *Risk of imitation:* exploit your advantage from going global *before* imitators can act to copy products, services, and processes.

4. *Risk of unsustainability:* generate sufficient payoffs *during* the leap to globalization to see the transformation through.

Recall that the relative intensity of each of these four risks determines the urgency of leaping: the higher the risks of elimination and exclusion if the company does not globalize, the greater the urgency to globalize; and the higher the risks of imitation and unsustainability if the company does globalize, the more difficult the leap will be. Nevertheless, our research shows that successful globalizers do not try to downplay or avoid the dangers of elimination, imitation, exclusion, and unsustainability. Rather they regard these risks as drivers and use them to accelerate the process of globalizing. Recognizing a principle from the Japanese martial arts at work in our data, we find that globalizers try to neutralize the impact of the threatening forces not by resisting them but by maneuvering in such a way as to draw out their energy and absorb them. This reversal of traditional attitudes toward risk appears simple, but it has important consequences for the ways globalizing companies operate.

Many of the more successful companies in our sample appear to match the four economic risks of globalization with four globalizing competences. These globalizing competences are skill sets that require highly capable people and thorough procedures to run at full steam. Because the leap to globalization affects the whole company, these competences need to become part of the fabric of daily activity. They can be thought of as engines, fueled by the four risks, for making the transformation to globalization. The greater the risk, the stronger its associated competence needs to be.

To address its risk of elimination from the newly forming global competitive game, the globalizing firm hones its ability to identify and capture business opportunities around the world. To respond to the risk of exclusion from resource partnerships and financial support networks, the globalizing firm articulates a global strategy that provides a compelling logic for business without borders. To counter the risk of imitation and obtain the best part of entrepreneurial profits, the globalizing firm implements its core business practices with precision and speed. Finally, to realize the cross-border economies necessary to support the globalizing investment and deal with the risk of unsustainability, the firm puts in place efficient growth management. Table 4.1 puts the risks of globalization and the corresponding globalizing competences side by side.

The following sections describe each globalizing competence in detail. We conclude the chapter with a discussion focused on the organizational structure required to integrate these competences.

Table 4.1. Risks of Globalization and Globalizing Competences.

Risks	Competences
Risk of elimination	Opportunity capture
Risk of exclusion	Global strategy articulation
Risk of imitation	Business practice implementation
Risk of unsustainability	Growth management

Risk of Elimination and Opportunity Capture

The risk of elimination implies a contest for market space. The globalizing company is racing to acquire all the new anywhere, anytime business around the world: winning customers, building market share, and achieving size to ward off predators. To counter the risk of elimination, the company needs to be able to attract as much new business as possible in a very short time frame.

Consider how Fresenius has managed the race for market space in consolidating the renal care and infusion nutrition sectors in health care. Whenever strategic acquisition opportunities have arisen, Fresenius has always seemed to come out the winner. In renal care, Fresenius solidified its U.S. market share by purchasing part of Abbott Laboratories' well-respected peritoneal dialysis (PD) equipment business. When NMC, the world's leading renal clinic operator, came up for sale a few years later, Fresenius managed to beat out its much bigger rival Baxter International in a hotly contested struggle. In infusion nutrition, the purchase of Kabi from Pharmacia & Upjohn in 1998 represents the culmination of Fresenius's drive for globalization, a strategy that was initiated with the 1992 acquisition of BASF Corporation's Knoll dialysis and infusion solution units and deepened with the 1997–98 purchase of Caremark's French, German, Dutch, and Canadian home care businesses (again outstripping Baxter).

What underlies this record of success in capturing opportunities in the face of significant competition? Fresenius managers are extremely well connected to decision makers in the industry and have been in the hunt for a number of years. In the case of the NMC acquisition, for example, CEO Gerd Krick had earlier offered to participate as a supporter of a management buyout at NMC (this buyout effort failed) well before the final showdown with Baxter. Baxter thought it was the only bidder and made a relatively uncompromising offer to NMC's owner, the W. R. Grace Corporation. But Krick came up with a better deal and personally sold it to Grace, the management of NMC, and the U.S. investment community. The story of the Kabi purchase from Pharmacia & Upjohn is similar: Fresenius made three separate top-management-led attempts at this purchase before succeeding. From top management on down, the people at Fresenius have a clear strategic orientation and a strong deal-making mentality: they know what they are after, have strong business contacts with suppliers and customers around the world that keep them apprised of fast-breaking opportunities, and are ready to act quickly and creatively.

Be at the right place at the right time and act on the advantage: easier said than done. Clearly, top-notch research is the first prerequisite. The globalizing competence of opportunity capture reflects the *intelligence* processes of a company. If the company is very good at opportunity capture, it has the processes in place to make it more intelligent than its competitors and is able to put its intelligence to the best use. To do research in markets it doesn't know from firsthand experience and on subjects that are notoriously hard to assess, like latent demand and company valuation, a company must build a network of strong connections. This network operates at *multiple* levels: CEO to CEO, local manager to local executive; and through intermediaries such as banks or consultants.

In the late 1980s, Spain-based Banco Santander established top-level personal ties with leading family-owned Latin American banks and installed investment bankers in each country so that it would know when, on whom, and how to pounce should the opportunity arise. Cemex has worked closely with one boutique New York investment bank to, first, research the highly fragmented and understudied cement sector and then systematically identify and deal for cement plants around the world. Aerospace and rolling stock leader Bombardier's current advance into Asia and Latin America is fronted by a concentrated effort to build business and governmental ties in the regions that are likely to be sources of new orders for the company's trains and planes. In all three companies, the investment in research and networking has been made without the prospect of an immediate payback. The objective, in the words of Bombardier's VP Robert Greenhill, is to get "eyes and ears on the ground."

Through research and networking, a company may be able to gain a time lead on the competition when going after new business opportunities. This lead proves useful in the race against elimination, however, only when organizational decision making is fast. Thus successful globalizers establish routines that permit proposals to pass quickly from the front line to top management and from top management to the board. At WorldCom, for example, capital investment procedures have been radically streamlined and standardized—so much so that the story of a $500 million European investment approved overnight is part of what WorldCom communications director Mark Weeks calls the "legend" of the company. According to Weeks, "the story shows what makes the company different from its ex-monopoly competitors." Similarly, Banco Santander could move to buy seven banks in as many weeks at the height of the 1995 Mexican peso crisis because entrepreneurs at Santander Investments had taken the initiative to build preparatory relationships *and* could call on bank headquarters in Madrid for a practically instantaneous response on purchase proposals. As one Santander Investments banker put it, "we have a direct line to [CEO] Emilio Botin."

Given that the opportunity capture competence revolves around knowledge gathering and decision-making processes, what kinds of people does the company need to master it? On the one hand, opportunity capture requires skills in acquiring local know-how, providing legal support, and conducting due diligence. It also requires deep operational expertise. These are the skills typically found in business developers at companies like Bombardier and CMS Energy and in operating subsidiary managers at companies like Fresenius and WorldCom. On the other hand, and perhaps even more important, opportunity capture depends on having managers with a deal-making mentality, an openness for new opportunities, a nose for the right price, and a drive for closure in negotiation. The globalizing company has to find and reward people who have an aptitude for deals. Bombardier's executive vice president Yvan Allaire says that his company "never uses investment banks in acquisitions." Clearly, not every company can manage opportunity capture entirely on its own. However, leaving this competence to outsiders prevents a company from developing know-how that may eventually prove crucial in its pursuit of globalization.

Opportunity capture is fueled by the risk of elimination, and managers need to act with a sense of urgency—"if we don't grab it, the others will." Without an opportunity capture competence in place, the leap to globalization either does not get off the ground at all or, more frequently, runs into early roadblocks as the first cut of customers and target acquisitions is creamed off by more nimble competitors. A broadly distributed opportunity capture competence is critical to staking a major claim during the initial gold rush. As the leap to globalization proceeds, the risk of elimination may recede somewhat (see Chapter Five), but opportunity capture continues to be important to the maintenance of a competitive position—there are always new customers to fight for, existing customers to pry loose from the competition, and acquisition possibilities to pursue.

Risk of Exclusion and Global Strategy Articulation

The leap to globalization both derives from and depends on resource partnerships. On the one hand, the presence of globalizing and already globalized partners drives globalization by raising the risk of exclusion. On the other hand, the help of others from related industries is essential in making the leap to globalization successfully. Suppliers, codevelopers, distributors, and investors—all put varying degrees of pressure on the company to globalize, and the company has to persuade them that it is up to the challenge and worthy of their cooperation. Successful globalizers do not resist exclusion partner by partner. Rather they develop a convincing *global strategy* to more readily *attract* partners.

According to Vic Fryling of CMS Energy, "In the beginning [of international expansion], you are not really strategic, you are opportunistic. Very early on [however], we came up with an idea we thought made us unique in the industry. . . . When you are heavily involved in a region, you should understand the energy market better than your competitors, and that should give you the advantage of seeing investment opportunities that others don't realize. . . . [We] are going from being a kind of investment house to really creating an integrated energy business." Once it has the outlines of a global strategy in place, the globalizer has, in effect, a *signature* that differentiates it from its competitors. This global strategy should be based upon sound economic reasoning. It should also explain to partners what is unique about the company's approach and specify how the company's international expansion steps add up to a whole that is more than the sum of the parts. Globalization has to show real benefits in terms of customer coverage, scale, and scope. For a while partners and particularly investors may be satisfied by a steady stream of new projects well implemented. Even data from the project-focused utility and telecommunications industries suggest, however, that this satisfaction is usually of short duration and that globalizers are eventually compelled to articulate a strategy. Partners want to see a logic that justifies long-term commitments—a logic that allows them to choose, quoting Vic Fryling's words about banks and investors, "a decent horse on which to bet."

A global strategy should also provide a rational explanation for the apparently irrational actions we have described in Chapter Three under the heading "Projection." We found that companies actively use their global strategies in this way to reduce the risk of exclusion. Thus Parmalat's decision to invest in a big way in North America makes sense in light of its global strategy of branded milk,

Bloomberg's early push into Japan follows from a global strategy of serving the major financial market players anywhere, and Infosys's establishment of a U.S. development beachhead is consistent with clearly stated ambitions to be the software provider of choice to large firms like Reebok and Citibank.

What does it mean to take on the risk of exclusion by articulating a global strategy? Externally, particularly vis-à-vis existing and prospective partners, global strategy articulation emphasizes a lucid and persuasive presentation of plans and achievements to date. The objective is to make the strategic trajectory look so attractive that potential partners feel compelled to work with the company. Before its collapse due to overambition and lack of oversight, Enron was known as the leading energy infrastructure trader in the world and attracted prime partners from a broad variety of sectors. How had the company gotten partners to buy into its unique approach of creating markets for infrastructure? Enron always tried to be the first one in with presentations to governments that were considering opening markets, it had been courting the financial community with detailed strategy presentations for much longer than its less dynamic rivals, and managed to plant gushing articles about itself in the business press with astonishing regularity. Similarly, World-Com's Bernie Ebbers missed no opportunity to explain the reasoning behind his company's leap to globalization, with a particular emphasis on explaining what makes his company's approach different from that of the former monopolies. When company stories go against prevailing industry wisdom, as they did for several years at Enron and WorldCom, it is even more important to get the tale across to skeptical audiences. Indeed, Gerd Krick argues that Fresenius's unique approach to renal care has "tipped the balance of contested acquisition bids" in the company's favor on several occasions. In clearly articulating global strategy, the globalizing company allays doubts and subdues critics, attracting partners to its vision.

Each partnering opportunity is an occasion to further the globalizing process and make sure that the company is on the right track. In other words, global strategy articulation cannot be concerned only with external presentation. Internally, the company must have processes in place to keep up a pattern of investment and action that is consistent with the externally articulated strategy. CMS Energy, for example, has changed the way it appraises new ventures. Specific hurdle rates are applied according to projects' strategic importance, thereby reducing the chances of success for nonstrategic projects. Bombardier's comprehensive, multilevel process ensures that all new developments meet standards for fit with the group's global aims. If a global strategy is to be implemented, people at all organizational levels have to know what it means in practical terms and see that decisions are taken to support its aims.

The global strategy articulation competence emphasizes commitment and consistency: it is the *big picture* competence. As such, global strategy articulation assumes major importance at critical turning points: at the start of the leap; on the occasion of major deals, make-or-break projects, and strategic shifts; and of course when signing up new partners. At all times during the leap, the global strategy question (does the whole add up to more than the sum of the parts?) should serve as a yardstick for the entire organization.

Risk of Imitation and Core Business Practice Implementation

Once the leap to globalization is under way and the company shows its value proposition to the world, imitators are increasingly likely to be drawn into the game. As we have discussed, the creation of value from globalization usually depends on business practices that are not well protected by patent or copyright: Fresenius's service to health insurers, for example, or Cemex's logistics and distribution system. These practices can be replicated, and competitors will try to do just that in a race that eventually goes to the company that becomes big enough to keep rivals out. This is why it is so important to implement effectively and quickly the business practices that support the drive to globalization.

The competence of business practice implementation concerns a company's capacity for *rapid action*. Globalization conceived of as anywhere, anytime value necessarily calls for standardization of core practices. Whether the company offers a product or a service, it is simply not possible for it to offer seamless access or to ramp up production and delivery quickly otherwise. What should be standardized to ensure rapid action? In answering this question, the company is not concerned as much with avoiding imitation (which is impossible) as it is with considering how to use the threat of imitation as an accelerator for globalizing.

Surprisingly perhaps, we found that successful leaps to globalization involve limited standardization. Resource consuming to implement and constraining on frontline entrepreneurship, standardization is restricted to core practices, those absolutely critical to putting in place the company's global value proposition. Different practices are critical in different companies. At Banco Santander, for example, financial systems and marketing are vital; at Ispat, turnaround savoir faire; at Starbucks, real-estate management and personnel choice. Fresenius has focused on acquisition integration, developing a few simple rules that define business practice transfer.

Identifying the right focus for the business practice implementation competence demands introspection and the ability to learn quickly from first experiences. In general, the leap to globalization sharply exposes strengths and weaknesses. A company can be world-class on only a few core practice dimensions, and they must be recognized relatively early.

Once core practices are identified, standardization is embodied in people and frequently also in written programs. In over half the cases we studied, dedicated teams from headquarters are sent into action on fresh projects and new acquisitions. These teams— SWAT teams in army parlance—consist of a few highly trained individuals who are dedicated to instilling a particular core practice, such as a certain approach to financial or manufacturing management, in the shortest time possible. Thus Ispat has a team of three highly experienced steel engineers who move from turnaround to turnaround, staying six to nine months to install Ispat's dry roll technology and set up new management processes. Banco Santander sends each new acquisition a team of five to ten financial system operatives from Madrid who set up the bank's accounting and information systems.

When starting up a plant, especially when it is the first one in a country, CMS Energy initially transfers experienced managers from an existing operating site to the new site. Rodney Boulanger, head of CMS's power business, stresses the importance of this mobility: "CMS International can just pick anybody in the company and send him to another country. If a subsidiary doesn't know how to deal with a partner, we send a guy who knows. He doesn't have to know everything about the local culture; all he has to do is to bring all his wonderful skills with him. He will be welcomed with open arms and everybody in the country will be subservient to this new person coming in because of his expertise."

Temporary forces of this type have to be good at operating and good at explaining how to operate. In addition, these experts have to be backed up and reinforced by written programs that are understandable and above all usable. One aspect of Bombardier's recent acquisition of rolling stock manufacturer Deutsche Waggonbau (DWA)—formerly owned by the East German state and privatized in 1995—illustrates how Bombardier's management practices are transferred increasingly rapidly to foreign acquisitions. As soon as the DWA takeover was completed, one of the top priorities was to transfer the Bombardier "Blue Book" bid review process. This is a tool used by all Bombardier Transportation subsidiaries to identify, evaluate, and price risks imbedded in rail contracts. "The adoption of the Blue Book methodology has been very fast at DWA," comments Eric Fournier, a transportation group vice president who plays an active role in such integrations. "In a little over eighteen months, the information included in DWA's reports has reached about 75 percent of the quality level achieved by North American subsidiaries, which have been using the process for decades." As Bombardier continues to expand internationally, targeting countries such as China, the swift transfer of its management systems will become increasingly important. Not only do tools like the Blue Book enable far-flung operations all to work to the same standards, they also help persuade the managers of acquired and partner companies of the value of doing things in the Bombardier way.

The growth competence of business practice implementation stresses the importance of rapid action and fosters a project mentality. In the leap to globalization, individual projects—customer start-ups, plant openings, acquisitions—are of critical importance. The globalizing company needs to bring its core practices to bear in these projects in order to distinguish itself from the competition at the operational level and maintain a margin for its global value proposition. Rather than running away from the risk of imitation, successful globalizers identify and implement core practices ahead of their rivals.

Risk of Unsustainability and Growth Management

As we have stressed, globalization is a double or quits game. It is not possible for a company to create new value from globalization and be only part global. The leap to globalization therefore entails the risk that the company will not get to its envisioned future safely: it may abandon its goal in midflight, be taken over, or fail. We have called this the risk of unsustainability. Although the ambition is to dominate the future, the leap to globalization has to pay back enough today to survive the present. Generating payoffs during the leap demands hard-nosed management of growth.

The globalizing competence of growth management can be thought of as the *supply line* of a campaign. Growth management maintains the functions that keep the leap going: exploitation of nascent scale economies, sharing of knowledge about developments around the world, financial management, and critically, strategic controls. Take the example of CMS Energy, a novice to international business. Within a short time after launching its leap to globalization, the company was pushing supplier Siemens for scale economies in the purchase of generating equipment, negotiating favorable relationships with major financial houses like Citibank on the basis of recent successes, and transferring Argentine managers to Venezuela in an effort to leverage skills in Latin American provincial government relations. Even more striking, CMS Energy has made international financial and political risk management a core practice.

As the CMS example illustrates, in order to generate sufficient payoffs en route to see the leap to globalization through, one of the things globalizers must do is carefully manage the cost side of their business. Because managing costs involves optimization of cross-country differences, globalizers can learn a lot from the best practices of leading multinationals like ABB, Procter & Gamble, and Sony. This is not to say that globalizers should organize like long-established global firms—this would be akin to trying to fit a tailored suit on an athlete in constant motion. But globalizers can use certain best practices of multinationals for their own objectives.

Not surprisingly, then, we find the presence of star hires from multinational companies in leading positions a striking feature of successful globalizers. Yahoo! has Tim Koogle; DoubleClick has Barry Salzman; Fresenius has Udo Werle; WorldCom has Liam Strong. The pedigrees of these managers read like a who's who of famous multinational companies: Motorola, McKinsey, ABB, British Airways. What roles do these *global managers* play?

The presence of one or more key global managers in companies that accomplish leaps to globalization is testimony to the truism that no leader can do it alone. However autocratic they may sometimes appear from the outside, leaders like Bernie Ebbers and Gerd Krick have delegated substantial authority. Global managers typically play central operational roles in making the promise of globalization a working reality in a company. They introduce best practices in the management of business across borders, ensuring that information systems, financial controls, and legal frameworks are suited to administer the complexity of a company seeking to jump-start in ten, twenty, or more country environments.

Although exiles from famous multinational companies are readily available, global managers are not a dime a dozen. Fresenius CFO Udo Werle, for example, has done a lot more than import practices and procedures. First and foremost, perhaps, global managers are teachers. Two younger finance operatives at Fresenius called Werle a "master, who taught us everything we know about information systems and financial decision making in a global company." By dint of their global living experiences and their personalities, global managers are able to convey to both novices and senior managers what it means to operate in a borderless environment: understanding differences in cultures and business routines is necessary of course, but more important is to have a strong sense of interdependence—to recognize the need for coordination across countries. Globalization implies that whatever one manager does in one place has implications for what other managers see and can do elsewhere. By personal example, through consultation on decisions, and through formal measures, global managers educate the people in the company about global interdependence.

Growth management and global managers dedicated to growth management are vital to sustaining the leap to globalization. Without strong growth management, there is every chance of coming up short. For example, had engineering giant Fluor put proper strategic controls in place at the outset of its leap rather than after globalizing projects lost money, we might well be talking about it as a globalization success story. As it is, the loss-making projects completely sapped shareholder confidence in the company's ability to succeed at globalization, and top management has had to significantly scale back its ambitions. In all the justified focus on creating new value from globalization, it should not be forgotten that the leap to globalization is a major growth management challenge and that costs must be closely controlled. Investors watch high-growth stories with an especially critical eye for evidence that the company is not up to managing the growth it has created. The downfall of Enron serves as a reminder that the proverbial plug is never far from their hands.

Competences Throughout the Organization

As the preceding examples show, globalizing competences are grafted onto the organization to deal with the risks inherent in the leap to globalization. However, we emphasize that these competences do not constitute a new or separate organization. Except in the special case of global start-ups, organizing the leap to globalization does not amount to reengineering the whole company. Table 4.2 sums up the key points to bear in mind about each competence: its role in the globalization process, what management area it concerns, how it is implemented, and who is involved.

Our data show that the globalizing competences are not centralized at corporate headquarters. Only global strategy articulation is the preserve of the executive office. The remaining competences are distributed throughout the organization. This finding raises the question of organizational structure in the globalizing company. We said earlier that globalizers generally do not adopt global structures as described in the existing literature, so we now need to specify how deal makers, core practice teams, senior executives, and global managers and the skills and attitudes they represent are integrated into the organization.

Focused Decentralization: A Management Approach for the Leap to Globalization

Any simple recipe for the management of a globalizing company will always fall afoul of the historical and cultural particularities of companies. No one size fits all when it comes to organizing an

Table 4.2. Characteristics of Globalizing Competences.

	Opportunity Capture	Global Strategy Articulation	Business Practice Implementation	Growth Management
Role	Intelligence	Signature	Rapid action	Supply line
What?	Research	Expansion path	Core practice	Control
How?	Decision making	Communication	Standardization	Teaching
Who?	Deal makers	Executive office	Expert teams	Global manager

entrepreneurial process. Nonetheless, some approaches may be more prone to success than others. In our research, *focused decentralization* emerges across contextual differences as a management approach well suited to organizing the leap to globalization.

Distribution of Competences and Decision Making Across Levels

Focused decentralization means that responsibility for key growth processes is shared across the organization. The term *decentralization* indicates that many managers, in their individual business and functional domains, contribute to the smooth running of the company's growth competences. The term *focused* indicates that these managers clearly understand the company's global objectives and have access to the requisite skills. Competence specialists and general managers across the company work hand in hand to make globalizing succeed.

Many other entrepreneurial processes require a concentration of decision making in the hands of one person. The leap to globalization does not appear to work this way. A single center of decision making performs the function of *absorbing* shocks far more slowly than numerous centers do. Sustaining the pace of growth typical of the race for globalization gold requires matching contributions from all over the company. No center can keep abreast of all the opportunities around the world and single-handedly maintain strategic consistency; no core practice or global manager can guarantee that seamless anywhere, anytime service is actually carried out. Corporate leadership and frontline entrepreneurship have to go together. Unless the managers taking anywhere, anytime value to the customer have considerable freedom to act, the leap to globalization may stall.

Once again, Fresenius offers a good example. In early 1993, frustrated by a variety of inconclusive consultant reports on strategy and organizational structure, Krick decided to reshape the company along market lines. He divided the divisions into self-managing units (*Unternehmen*) and made every unit manager (*Unternehmer*) strictly responsible for the performance of his or her own business. Between the *Unternehmen* a strict regime of arm's length contracting obtains. Even the use of support functions is charged to the *Unternehmer*, and he or she has the option to go outside the company for anything and to anybody, including the competitors of Fresenius. Each *Unternehmer* is judged on strict earnings growth targets, and sizeable bonuses ride on the ability to meet these targets.

This *Unternehmer im Unternehmen* structure has been important in putting globalizing competences into action and speeding up Fresenius's expansion. According to Krick, the NMC deal would have been "unthinkable, without the *Unternehmer* structure." However, because Fresenius's dialysis products business was already in effect independent, it was relatively easy to combine it with NMC and establish a new company.

The decentralized process embodied in the *Unternehmer* structure has proven very effective in focusing managers' attentions. Within days of the announcement of the significant Kabi acquisition in 1998, for example, the *Unternehmer* at Fresenius took the initiative to telephone their counterparts at Kabi around the world with a view to starting coordination discussions. The *Unternehmer* are also instrumental in identifying new growth opportunities, with a simple, streamlined process for getting their expansion and investment proposals directly to top management. Thanks to the introduction of the *Unternehmer* structure, according to Krick, the company has been able "for the first time in its history" to increase sales without a corresponding increase in headcount.

Implementation of the *Unternehmer* principle occurred in two steps: it was introduced first in Germany and then on a divisional basis abroad. Matthias Schmidt, who directs Fresenius's Kabi division, notes that the transition was actually harder for home country managers than for foreign subsidiary heads: the latter had always been operating in a de facto entrepreneurial setting. In every foreign country in which Fresenius has business, there is at least one *Unternehmer* per division, with larger divisional operations (such as NMC in the United States) subdivided among several *Unternehmer*.

The *Unternehmer* of the division with the highest sales in a country also serves as country head, acting, in Krick's words, as a "hotel keeper who provides and charges for legal and administrative assistance" but who has no business authority over the other *Unternehmer*. Every *Unternehmer* acts as a kind of mini-CEO, having both broad responsibilities and a deep appreciation of where the company as a whole is going. Theoretically each business could be used as a basis on which to recreate the whole company. The Fresenius plant manager in Schweinfurt, Germany, and the Fresenius sales manager in São Paulo represent equivalent management values, work with the same organizational processes, and pursue complementary objectives.

Fresenius's management practices are particularly instructive because this company structure was developed to accompany the process of globalization. In most of the other organizations in our research sample, structural change did not occur. It turned to be more cost efficient and effective to spread out the competences required for the process of globalizing than to overhaul the organization. In companies like CMS Energy, Gemplus, Bombardier, and Cemex, the globalizing process was grafted on to the existing structure.

Knowledge of Strategy and Payoff Control

In the absence of a new structure, what ensures consistency in the various actions of the frontline managers charged with implementing the globalizing competences? Globalization is an entrepreneurial process that is highly innovative and therefore has to admit a certain amount of disorder, but too much disorder does a disservice to concentrated effort. The question of coordination between center and periphery is one of the persistent issues in managing decentralized processes, and there are no simple solutions. Our research identified two managerial anchors for maintaining consistency in decentralization: knowledge of strategy and payoff control.

Knowledge of strategy throughout the company is critical. Decentralization works when frontline managers know precisely what the company is trying to achieve. This requires clear leadership of the globalization effort from the top, supporting input from a cadre of global managers, and standardized core practices, as described earlier in this chapter.

Ultimately, knowledge and acceptance come from participation, and the leap to globalization is very often accompanied by an intensification of the strategy-making process across all levels. This means that time is devoted to globalization strategy and to fundamental strategic debate, even, and especially, for people such as project developers in utilities like CMS Energy and plant managers in manufacturers like Cemex or Bombardier. A sound strategy process helps ensure that decentralization does not dissolve into anarchy.

Practices at Bombardier show how far a company can go to vitalize the strategy process. Group heads and, in turn, division managers are given great entrepreneurial freedom but within a web of checks and balances such as financial controls, strategic planning processes, incentive systems driven by Economic Value Added™, succession plans, and program reviews. Jean-Yves Leblanc, president and chief operating officer of Bombardier Transportation, explains how decision making trickles down the corporate echelons:

> I am responsible for my Group's results and have the mandate to do whatever is needed to ensure profitable growth. I am spending half of my time on issues like bid reviews, setting and monitoring performance targets, coordinating interbusiness activities, channeling R&D efforts, and developing resources and talent. Most operational activities, such as marketing, strategy implementation, client service, and manufacturing excellence, for instance, are now the daily bread of the heads of my four profit centers [North America, Latin America, Atlantic Europe, and Continental Europe]. I keep a constant dialogue with these managers, both informally and formally, via a series of reviews running throughout the year. I also talk to Mr. Beaudoin [the chairman] on a regular basis, both informally and through our monthly and quarterly reviews. But our most vigorous discussions are certainly channeled through the planning process. These are not mere information sessions, like planning meetings

turn into for many companies. Only the people strictly necessary to the discussions are allowed in and talks are very, very intense. Guys like Laurent Beaudoin, Paul Larose [CFO], and Yvan Allaire [executive vice president, strategy] ask the tough questions, challenge your assumptions, and look you straight in the eyes when you answer.

In short, the independence of local decision makers with regard to means is counterbalanced by a reporting system that demands strict adherence to commitments and focuses on results.

Focused decentralization is not the natural choice of the entrepreneur. Thus at some companies, the globalization effort remains the preserve of a visionary executive (supported by an ad hoc team) who tries to persuade the company to go global while holding on tightly to all aspects of the globalization effort. This separation of globalization and business as usual plays to the nonglobal history of the company and attempts to circumvent inertia. However, our research shows that it is precisely the opposite approach that is associated with success in globalizing: the more decentralized the activity centers of a globalizing company, the more complete the leap. Bombardier chairman Laurent Beaudoin, for example, sees his role as being "the conductor of an orchestra. . . . I don't play all the instruments, but I can tell you when they're playing in tune" (Holloway, 1999, p. 162).

The focused decentralization approach works only when each unit, and by implication each manager, is at one with the globalization objective of the company. If the strategy of globalization by leap is clearly explained and unmistakably backed up by executive action and payoff-oriented control systems, managers in the field will be their own best supervisors. Note that the explanation of strategy corresponds to the competence of global strategy articulation and that the payoff-oriented control system is an integral part of the growth management competence. In other words, not only do the globalizing competences directly address the risks encountered in globalizing, they also help ensure the coherence of decentralized entrepreneurship in the pursuit of the globalization objective (see Figure 4.1).

Figure 4.1. Organizing the Leap to Globalization.

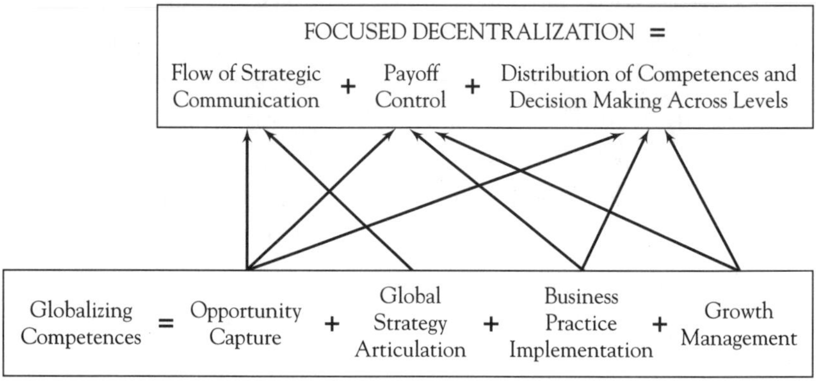

In its basic shape the successful globalizing organization is not necessarily radically new and certainly not global or transnational in any standard sense. Better adapted to the leap growth process than any single "right" organizational structure, the globalizer's absorption of risks by means of specialized competences ensures that the globalizer is able to act with great force and singularity of purpose.

Conclusion

In this chapter, we have described what the globalizing organization looks like during its leap to globalization. Successful globalizers engage in a process of absorbing the risks inherent in the leap. Rather than trying to avoid the risks of elimination, exclusion, imitation, and unsustainability, companies like Fresenius and Bombardier become skilled in applying globalizing competences that turn the risks into sources of advantage. The absorption of risk works at two levels: first, in the integration of a set of support mechanisms (globalizing competences) into the fabric of the organization and, second, in the use of a focused decentralization approach that ensures the entrepreneurial process is coherently pursued throughout the company and not concentrated at corporate headquarters.

Absorption of Risks = Globalizing Competences
+ Focused Decentralization

On the basis of our research at Fresenius, Bombardier, and other successful globalizers, we pose three questions that executives at globalizing companies can use to test whether their organization is supportive of the globalizing process:

1. Given the importance of responding to risk with globalizing competences, is there a sufficient number of managers in the company with the power to act individually on

   - Opportunity capture?
   - Strategy articulation?
   - Practice implementation?
   - Growth management?

2. Are these managers adequately spread out to touch all the company's vital areas?

3. Do these managers have a clear understanding of the thinking and resources behind the company's leap to globalization?

In our experience, the organizational causes for failure in globalizing take two forms:

- Top management does not understand that the risks of globalization have to be systematically transformed into globalizing competences. Instead, executives either block progress or try to deny the existence of risks. With this mentality, each step toward globalization gives rise to internal mini-crises that revisit the risks and substantially slow down the process.

- Top management does not decentralize enough; executives keep the process of globalizing to themselves and their staffs. When conditions change, the company is slow to react, and executives complain about "inertia." Inertia of this kind is a matter of management, and it can be addressed with focused decentralization that spreads responsibility for the globalizing process.

To be sure, success stories like WorldCom and Starbucks did not simply emerge as full-blown globalizers, with globalizing competences and focused decentralization in place. Neither are these two companies or most other globalizers making it through the leap to globalization without ups and downs. Globalizing competences and focused decentralization are necessary to develop momentum but not sufficient to maintain the leap in the face of serious challenges along the way. How do thriving globalizers align skills and negotiate challenges along the road to world leadership?

We have not yet explicitly addressed the timing of key organizational activities. *When* do companies build globalizing competences? Timing, of course, is also about follow-through, and we also need to look at *how* companies can maintain globalizing competences. In the next chapter, we analyze the leap of the globalizer over time.

Chapter Five

Harmonization

Adapting to Changing Risks Over Time

In the preceding chapters we described *projection* and *absorption*—the strategic and organizational imperatives in a successful leap to globalization. We showed how both *acting "as if"* globalization were already in place at the outset of the leap and putting in place specialized competences to deal with the risks of the globalizing process are necessary supports for a company's transformation from national or multinational to global. We have also pointed out that the word *leap* implies a rapid process. Indeed our observation that a number of companies have globalized very quickly had a lot to do with our initial interest in researching globalization. Recall Gemplus's expansion to forty countries in five years and WorldCom's spectacular emergence from 1996 to 1999 as a key provider of anywhere, anytime service for the likes of Shell and Ford. In this chapter, then, we address the issue of time and related questions about pace and momentum. In particular, we focus on the manner in which the companies in our research sample managed the evolution of globalizing risks over the course of their leaps.

It is not sufficient to say that time is important and that the globalizing process today takes place with unprecedented speed. Executives need to understand how globalizers manage speed. We found that the leap to globalization is not a process that obeys traditional notions of time and order. Many of the successful companies we studied had defied analysts' dire warnings of "too much, too soon." Even more intriguingly, they succeeded not by sticking to rote plans and simply multiplying a formula across countries but by flexibly adapting to changing circumstances.

We use the term *harmonization* to capture this flexible adaptation to changing circumstances in the globalizing process. Harmonization denotes the globalizer's ability to recognize and then *respond to* (harmonize with) its environment and the concomitant competitive risks. The successful globalizer anticipates the need for change and adjusts its priorities accordingly. This ability contrasts with the organizational inertia associated with the typical business enterprise. Globalization is about projection and bets on the future *and* about absorption and specialized competences *and*, perhaps most crucially, about taking an opportunistic approach to managing priorities over time.

The Phases of Globalizing

Generally speaking, the leap to globalization has two phases: a *conquering-new-markets* phase and a *protecting-existing-business* phase. The conquering-new-markets phase—which might involve deregulation or technology adoption at the time when the globalizing process is just getting under way—is characterized by the search for first mover advantage. A protecting-existing-business phase—which might involve industry consolidation or major acquisition integration—is characterized by the search for efficiency gains. In terms of timing, initial conquering precedes protecting. However, and this is a critical observation from our research, a phase of protecting may be followed by a new phase of conquering and that phase may be followed by yet another phase of protecting. In practice, conquering and protecting alternate and overlap.

This finding has clear implications for management. It suggests that management must alternate over time between emphasizing development and emphasizing control. This alternation can also be stated in terms of globalization risks and globalizing competences. Opportunity capture and global strategy articulation, the competences corresponding to the risks of elimination and exclusion that prompt the company to make the leap in the first place, are emphasized during the process of finding, attracting, and signing new business. Opportunity capture and global strategy articulation can therefore be called the *development competences* for making the leap to globalization. Business practice implementation and growth management, the globalizing competences corresponding to the risks of imitation and unsustainability, are emphasized when it is necessary to control the course of expansion. They can be called the *competences of control*. Each set of competences will be more or less important depending on the phase—development or control—the globalizing company is currently going through. The relationships between the phases of growth, globalizing risks, and competence priorities are summarized in Figure 5.1.

A simple phase model with a predefined sequence of steps cannot accurately describe the globalizing process. On the contrary, successful globalization appears to require a specific approach to managing path dependency. The individual phases of growth turn out to be less important than the transitions between them. Two means of overcoming organizational inertia have helped the successful globalizers to navigate these transitions: first, a countercyclical approach to building globalizing competences and, second, a flexible approach to the administrative hierarchy.

Figure 5.1. Phases, Risks, and Competences.

	Development Phase	Control Phase
Globalizing Risks	Elimination Exclusion	Imitation Unsustainability
Competence Priorities	Opportunity capture Strategy Articulation	Practice implementation Growth management

A Countercyclical Approach to Building Globalizing Competences

When we looked at the juxtaposition in time between key resource decisions to build globalizing competences and dominant risks in the environment, we found that the companies we studied often made decisions to invest in competences *before* they had an objective need for those competences. In other words, successful companies build up globalizing competences before changes in the competitive situation suggested the need for corresponding changes in risk priority and growth emphasis. Consider, for example, the competence investment patterns at Fresenius, CMS Energy, and Gemplus, our three lead research sites.

In phases of development and conquering new markets, where the risk of elimination is highest, Fresenius's key resource decisions for the future have appeared to concern growth management (Table 5.1). In phases of control and protecting gains, where the risk of unsustainability is highest, key resource decisions for the future have concerned opportunity capture. The hiring from ABB of CFO Udo Werle, the global manager who was to have a major influence on systems and processes for cross-country coordination in the company, came at a time when globalization and the attendant scramble for opportunities was just getting under way. The development of a business model for disease state management (DSM), in order to partner with insurance companies, followed shortly on the heels of the NMC acquisition, when everyone from business analysts to bankers was worrying about Fresenius's ability to sustain its globalization drive. During the period of the company's greatest deal-making euphoria, surrounding the acquisition of Kabi from Pharmacia, Krick and Werle were already investing in state-of-the-art SAP enterprise resource planning (ERP) systems to buffer the oncoming control phase of globalization, and in 2000, as the game appeared won, Fresenius was assembling new skills in business development to strengthen its position and prepare it to go further afield.

Table 5.1. Building Globalizing Competences: Fresenius.

	Date			
	Q1 1993	Q2 1995	Q2 1998	Q2 2000
Context	Globalization starts	NMC purchase	Kabi purchase	Refocusing
Principal current risk	Elimination	Unsustainability	Elimination	Unsustainability
Key resource decision for the future	Hiring of Udo Werle as CFO	Development of new disease state management plan	Transition to SAP enterprise resource planning	Hiring of new doctors and deal makers

A very similar pattern of countercyclical resource decisions can be observed at CMS Energy (Table 5.2). Here, all four globalization risks take turns at center stage, and the analysis indicates how a relatively successful globalizer responds to temporary setbacks. Countercyclical resource decisions are used not only to build globalizing competences in advance of need but also to differentiate the company from competitors. As discussed in Chapter Three, COO Vic Fryling saw CMS becoming the "world's foremost regional energy integrator." The pursuit of this strategy required thinking ahead and doing things differently. Thus, when competitors like National Power, Tractebel, and even AES were measuring success only in terms of deals signed, CMS was building financial risk management competences that would allow the company to maintain coherence in a widely dispersed set of projects. As competitors were being forced by investors to get a better handle on risk, CMS was moving to articulate a global strategy that would make it a very attractive partner for energy infrastructure financiers the world over. By the time competitors were talking strategy (as National Power did in spring 1999), CMS had already moved to implement a growth management policy that tied new projects strictly to the company's

Table 5.2. Building Globalizing Competences: CMS Energy.

	Date			
	Q2 1993	Q3 1995	Q2 1998	Q1 2000
Context	Globalization starts	First string of deals in Latin America	World-leading energy projects	Sector profits low
.Principal current risk	Elimination	Imitation	Exclusion	Unsustainability
Key resource decision for the future	Hiring of Al Wright as CFO	Global strategy put in place	New project policy revised	Tracking stock proposed

ability to realize broader regional or cross-country gains. Even in the face of dwindling profits in the utility sector, CMS tried to break with the norm. It proposed a tracking stock for its high-growth, deregulated non-U.S. business. Although this last countercyclical decision backfired and had to be withdrawn in the face of investor criticism, CMS continues to look for new ways to get ahead of the pack. Ease of imitation in energy infrastructure means that the company must try continuously to differentiate its value proposition.

At Gemplus (Table 5.3), countercyclical resource decisions even have a metaphor of their own: to Marc Lassus, an avid surfer, it is a matter of "catching the next wave, before it catches you." We make our point here through examining one key resource decision and the attendant transition of growth emphasis. In 1997, Gemplus was in the middle of a singularly successful expansion drive, opening up new markets and new offices by the dozen every year and articulating a powerful new global strategy. Clearly, development was at the top of the company's agenda. The only way to be aware of a coming phase change is to look at nondevelopment indicators, the internal control competences. How good is the company at business practice implementation? At growth management?

At Gemplus in the mid-1990s, the capability to deliver on the core service proposition of security solutions anywhere, anytime did

Table 5.3. Building Globalizing Competences: Gemplus.

	Date			
	Q2 1990	Q3 1994	Q4 1997	Q4 2000
Context	Globalizing start-up	Production in 10 countries	Technology and market change	Margin pressure
Principal current risk	Elimination	Imitation	Exclusion	Unsustainability
Key resource decision for the future	Manufacturing optimized	Alliance strategy launched	Hiring of Pat Jones as CFO	New tech group under chairman

not match the promise. Moreover, potential scale economies were not being achieved, and knowledge about customers was inadequately shared. From the analysis of Chapter Two, we know that the risks of imitation and unsustainability are high in absolute terms for Gemplus. However, as long as the risks of imitation and unsustainability were *relatively* small compared to the risks of elimination and exclusion, these deficiencies did not warrant a radical refocusing of attention. By 1997 the entry of significant rivals (such as IBM) and the emergence of truly global customers such as Citibank had substantially raised the risks of imitation and unsustainability relative to the risks of elimination and exclusion. Under these changed conditions, practice implementation and growth management deficiencies could put the survival of the company in jeopardy. Gemplus CEO Marc Lassus understood and acted upon these challenges by installing a new chief financial officer, in preparation for taking the company into a new phase of protecting existing business and pursuing control. In announcing the appointment to employees, Lassus pointed out the need for adjusting emphasis, "It's like a high-performance sports car. To get from 60 mph to 100 mph, you must take your foot off the gas for a moment to change gears."

Beyond Fresenius, CMS, and Gemplus, our research sample contains many other examples of a countercyclical approach to building globalizing competences. Thus Banco Santander installed opportunity driven deal makers in Latin America in the late 1980s in preparation for a race for banking acquisitions. Subsequently, during the phase of accelerated opportunity capture (1994 to 1996), Banco Santander perfected sophisticated financial systems that would allow it to monitor the risks of its new outposts. Bombardier invested in building a new strategic architecture and control systems during the same period that the company went on an acquisition spree that brought eight new businesses into the fold in five years. This countercyclical investment in growth management competence readied the firm to capitalize on its new network.

A Flexible Approach to Administrative Hierarchy

Reading and recognizing change is one thing, fast, united reaction quite another. A principal difficulty in managing the process of globalizing is that even when some leaders have a opportunistic conception of time, most managers in the field do not. The former may understand that the sequencing of actions is dependent on circumstances and therefore subject to change, whereas the latter are used to linear evolution and its attendant effect of irreversibility. This difficulty is especially pronounced when management hierarchy is at issue. Leaders involved in globalizing would like to be able to keep the hierarchical order flexible, altering the pecking order of the globalizing competences as needed. Having a different conception of time, more traditional managers do not understand why the hierarchical order, once established, should be questioned.

It is illusory to imagine that the *whole* company will develop a shared conception of time as it relates to change. This conception will be difficult even for those managers implementing the globalizing competences. They too are liable to succumb to inertia, defending the status quo once it is put in place. For example, SWAT teams entrusted with business practice implementation are likely to demand more and more resources when the risk of imitation is high.

However, in the countercyclical approach to resource decisions, a period of increasing risk of imitation is precisely the time for initiating investment in the globalizing competences of development—opportunity capture and global strategy articulation—competences that may not seem necessary to the SWAT teams implementing core business practices.

Managing resource decisions countercyclically clearly requires great attention to the application of these decisions. We do not believe there are any general rules to follow to prevent battles for influence and the defense of self-interest. Depending on their histories and their leaders, some companies will be better equipped than others to deal with internal divisions arising from changes in competence emphasis. Through our research, we have tried to understand the management approaches under which the different globalizing competences can be made to harmonize with respect to both changing competitive conditions and the less malleable predispositions of actors internal to the organization.

Focused decentralization can work very well on its own when the strategic direction of the company is set and the globalizing competence emphasis is defined. This is the *fly-by-wire* type of system that Krick has instituted at Fresenius: the *Unternehmer* have considerable freedom in their own domain but follow well-established, company-level objectives. Once set in motion this kind of system is relatively responsive to smaller shocks but does not adjust to major upheavals without significant modification. Therefore focused decentralization alone is not sufficient as a management approach in a truly dynamic globalization context.

Successful globalizers, we have found, negotiate the ups and downs of the leap by supplementing decentralization with a hierarchy of objectives that adapts with changing risks, permitting rapid responses over time but not compromising the power of decentralization. In a flexible hierarchy of objectives, the relative standing of development managers and control managers is explicitly adapted to changing conditions. If control has to be king for a time, for example, then the CFO becomes the real boss (as happened at Gemplus), operations sit in on development strategy (as happened at CMS Energy), and everyone focuses on cost control (as happened at WorldCom). Conversely, if a reading of change indicates that development has to become king, deal makers take charge and innovation becomes the watchword. In these ways, decentralization is complemented by a flexible, revolving hierarchy.

Tables 5.4, 5.5, and 5.6 illustrate how Fresenius, CMS Energy, and Gemplus implemented the flexible hierarchy concept over time. Priority shifts among globalizing competences go hand in

Table 5.4. Implementing Flexible Hierarchy: Fresenius.

	Date			
	1993–1995	1995–1996	1996–1998	1998–2000
Context	Globalization starts	NMC purchase	Kabi purchase	Refocusing
Dominant competence	Opportunity capture	Growth management	Opportunity capture	Growth management
Implementation	*Unternehmer* structure put in place	*Unternehmer* "learn" finance from Werle	*Unternehmer* given active role in new mergers and acquisitions	*Unternehmer* subjected to group incentives

Table 5.5. Implementing Flexible Hierarchy: CMS Energy.

	Date			
	1993–1995	1995–1997	1997–1999	1999–2001
Context	Globalization starts	First string of deals in Latin America	World-leading energy projects	Sector profits low
Dominant competence	Opportunity capture	Finance practice implementation	Global strategy articulation	Growth management
Implementation	Developers have top-level support and freedom	Plant and project managers have direct line to top	External reps have first call on resources	Developers submit to new strategic criteria

hand with concrete managerial actions. At Fresenius, the flexible hierarchy finds expression in changes in the focus of the *Unternehmer* structure around which the organization is built. At CMS Energy, different functions take center stage in the different phases of the company's expansion drive. At Gemplus, concrete strategic or personnel moves give rise to adjustments in the hierarchy of globalizing competences.

Note the striking correspondence between development and control phases as discussed earlier and adjustments in the hierarchy of globalizing competences. The position of a competence is tied to the priority of risks: when the risk of elimination is highest, Fresenius puts deal making at the top of the *Unternehmer*'s agenda; CMS Energy gives full support and freedom to developers; and Gemplus emphasizes sales and new offices above all else. Conversely, when the risk of unsustainability assumes priority, Fresenius stresses financial management for the *Unternehmer*, CMS Energy puts developers under strategic control, and Gemplus hands over the reins of the company to CFO Pat Jones and his team of finance specialists.

Internal harmonization between risks and competences requires a comprehensive approach to implementation. Top management— the leader of the charge—has to communicate the urgency of the change with insistence and make convincing signals. In Gemplus's

Table 5.6. Implementing Flexible Hierarchy: Gemplus.

	Date			
	1990–1994	1994–1996	1996–1998	1998–2000
Context	Globalizing start-up	Production in 10 countries	Technology and market change	Margin pressure
Dominant competence	Opportunity capture	Business practice implementation	Global strategy articulation	Growth management
Implementation	Overriding focus on sales and new offices	Factory managers have say on mix and time	Alliance strategy pursued at all levels	Pat Jones put in charge; new CEO installed

1997 to 1998 transition to a control emphasis, Marc Lassus refocused his presentations around the issues of margin and cost and went out and hired Pat Jones, a finance specialist with the credibility bonus of a great career at Intel. Perhaps just as important for the successful shift of emphasis at Gemplus, Lassus himself stepped away from operating responsibilities and the CEO position shortly after Pat Jones came on board. He reinforced the move to a control emphasis by appointing as the new CEO Daniel LeGal, a highly analytical professional manager. With the ground thus prepared, Pat Jones could introduce tools and policies that required significant changes in the company's decision-making processes and have those tools and policies met with open arms. As Jones once explained, "It's scary—there's been no resistance. . . . Our employees are saying, 'Please give us the rules.' . . . They want to do the right thing to make the company succeed."

The right signals can recalibrate the balance among competences. The arrival of Pat Jones at Gemplus, for example, effectively indicated the promotion of the control competences (and the finance function) to the position of first among equals and the demotion of the development competences. Without concrete *actions*, however, signals can lose their influence quickly. It is important to follow up communication and signals with actions that enforce a change of emphasis both in competences and in individual job briefs. At Gemplus, each region was newly staffed with financial managers reporting directly to Jones. With the emphasis on the control phase and the growth management competence, developers at CMS Energy have to countenance operations managers in new project approval meetings and show higher rates of return for projects that do not clearly fit the company's global strategy. When WorldCom moves into a phase to be dominated by growth management (as it did after the MCI acquisition), individual incentives are adjusted to deemphasize deal making and support cost control.

Of course even a comprehensive approach to implementation that covers communication, signals, and concrete actions cannot prevent difficulties in maintaining a flexible hierarchy. In phases dominated by development concerns, control specialists may feel that the company is literally growing out of control; in phases of control dominance, business developers may lose interest and leave the company. We observed both of these extremes in our research.

Executives need to make every effort to take the drama out of not being "first" all the time and avoid having managers feel disavowed by shifts in emphasis. In effect, top management needs to instill a spirit of *modesty* that obliges every manager to think about the other globalizing competences before thinking about his or her own. Executives encourage this kind of modesty in practice when they keep managers informed about the issues facing all the competences and invite exchanges of ideas across specialist boundaries. At CMS Energy, for example, developers and controllers sit together on investment review committees that cover global strategy concerns beyond the managers' direct purview. These committees purposely include managers from regions with differing perspectives.

It is important that both those managers with control and those with development competences understand that maintaining the process of the leap will require changes that are in effect promotions and demotions. The group that feels underappreciated at the moment of a change in emphasis must remember that its time will come. Again, executives bear the primary responsibility for selling the growth story of the company, so that people will believe and make sacrifices. This internal storytelling is as important as the globalizing company's external presentation of itself.

Making Harmonization Work

Harmonization is the indispensable third management imperative in the process of globalizing by leap. Harmonization, our research shows, is not a simple reaction to today's circumstances; rather it implies an ability to exploit a time lag between risk in the future and competence buildup in the present. The company that waits until a risk is full-blown before it invests in building up the corresponding competence is creating a major impediment to continued growth. Harmonization is the means by which management adapts company strategy and organization to a context that is evolving along with the globalizing company. In particular, operating the four globalizing competences simultaneously but at changing individual intensities is an art that can be mastered only with a malleable, opportunistic conception of time. This conception of time is the basis on which management changes priorities among competences as necessary and develops acceptance of a continuously flexible hierarchy of objectives.

> Harmonization = Countercyclical Approach
> + Flexible Hierarchy

For a leap to globalization to succeed, development and control competences, like left and right limbs of the body, have to pull in the same direction. Too many new developments pursued and not enough attention to control, and disaster results. Not enough new development and too much emphasis on control, and momentum is lost. As the environment and the relative importance of the different globalization risks change over time, the relationship between the different globalization competences needs to change also. Because there is no way to hold the risks constant, the globalizing company has to continuously reevaluate its priorities and be ready to make necessary adjustments. Clearly, having reliable indicators of changes in the relative importance of the risks of globalization is critical. Table 5.7 offers sets of questions that executives can ask to help them identify such changes.

Reading the evolution of relative risk intensities accurately is difficult and hard to systematize. There will always be an element of hunch or feeling in interpreting often conflicting signals. The approach we propose brings external and internal data together to provide a nuanced picture of the company's expansion trajectory. The success of a leap to globalization ultimately depends on both the ability to develop and control and the ability to switch back and

Table 5.7. Questions to Identify Changes in the Relative Importance of Risks.

Risk of Elimination	Risk of Exclusion	Risk of Imitation	Risk of Unsustainability
• Are we facing New demands? New competitors? Poorer terms?	• Are we facing New partners? New approaches? New terms?	• What is our ability to Protect core processes? Transfer best practice? Replicate quickly?	• What is our level of New investment? Economies realized? Information shared?
• Is the game the same?	• Who sets the rules?	• Can we deliver on our promises?	• Are we focused on strategic control?
Questions concern the nature of the market for products and services.	*Questions concern the nature of the resource exchange.*	*Questions concern the ability to put business practices in place.*	*Questions concern the ability to exploit economies.*

forth between development and control emphases according to the circumstances. For the companies we studied, the leap to globalization was not an easily mapped out step-by-step affair. They have had to adjust their priorities in line with changes in the business environment.

In arguing for harmonization, we stress the need to read change by antithetical reasoning, to ask control questions in a phase of new market conquest, and to ask development questions in a phase of existing business protection. Figure 5.2 is a graphical reminder of the model introduced in this chapter.

Although powerful if exercised with the right timing, counter-cyclical resource decisions alone are not sufficient to ensure that the globalizing company adjusts to changing risk intensities. With control and development phases following each other in succession over the course of the leap to globalization, the organizational hierarchy also has to adapt continuously. As we have seen, not all of the globalizing competences are equally critical to the leap all of the time. As competitive conditions shift, the relative intensities of the globalizing risks are altered. The hierarchy of globalizing competences in turn has to harmonize with changes in globalizing risks. There will be phases during the leap when one set of globalizing competences or the other—development or control—needs to assume primary importance in the growth calculus of the company.

Figure 5.2. Countercyclical Approach to Building Globalizing Competences.

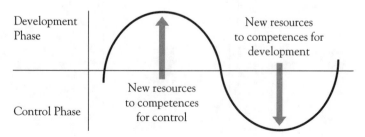

To install and manage a flexible hierarchy, the company needs to know how to read contextual changes and how to adjust the globalizing competences in response.

Over time and during the course of the leap to globalization, the relative intensity of globalization risks changes. Changes in relative risk intensity are not easily predicted and do not always follow in the same order. That is why the concept of harmonization captures the reality of the globalizer better than does a phase model with a set sequence of steps.

Conclusion

Executives who apply the concept of harmonization effectively understand that the process of globalizing is never linear. In our research experience, the process becomes blocked when harmonization is not achieved for either of these two reasons:

- The executive puts off action on strategy and organization in the (ultimately vain) hope of hitting on the one best way of globalizing, failing to come to grips with the impossibility of perfection in a context of constant change.
- The executive has an opportunistic conception of time but clashes irreconcilably with the conservatism of managers defending acquired positions of strength, and precious time is wasted in battles over turf.

We have stressed that the executive's role in harmonization consists of telling the globalization story and sending organizational signals that encourage managers on the front line to *live* a flexible hierarchy, understanding that their ultimate influence grows when they can accept a temporary reduction of emphasis on their personal competences for the greater good.

Exhibit 5.1 offers a test for a company's overall globalizing readiness.

Exhibit 5.1. A Test: Are You Ready to Leap?

Today there is new opportunity in globalization. Across a wide variety of industries, some of the most successful companies of the last five years have embraced this opportunity and grown at tremendous rates. The leap to globalization represents a great management challenge. It is not easy to get off the ground; far-reaching organizational changes have to be made, and adjustments over time play a critical role. Chapters Three, Four, and Five have drawn a composite picture of the successful leap. We now invite the practitioner to reflect on the following questions in order to test his or her company's preparedness to globalize or, if it is already engaged in globalizing, its management of that process.

Projection: Action

1. How can the company create new value from globalization?

2. Are executives willing to make unconventional bets on the future?

3. Do the people at the top have the courage to lead the charge?

Absorption: Organizing

4. Has the company built four superior competences for globalizing?

5. Are responsibilities fully delegated for quick, autonomous decision making?

6. Is the strategy clearly defined, well communicated, and supported by appropriate reporting systems?

Harmonization: Time

7. Are resource decisions taken with a view to countering the cycles of risk?

8. Will people readily accept changes in competence priorities?

Working out the answers to these questions will put the company on the right path for managing the leap to globalization. It is of course unlikely that any practitioner will be able to respond to every question in the affirmative before launching the leap. Our research experience tells us, however, that every globalizer has to face these questions sooner or later.

Chapter Six

The Leap to Globalization

A Synthesis

In the preceding chapters, we examined the entrepreneurial process of leaping to globalization. We looked at it part by part, carefully distinguishing the entrepreneurial process that leads to globalization from the organization of the global company. We found that globalizing is best understood not as a one-time collective transformation but as an evolutionary process that a company's leaders superimpose on the existing organization. That is why we do not speak of a clearly defined, static *before* and *after*. The successful leap to globalization is a result of a consistent set of actions that operate over time to change both the strategy and the management of the globalizing company. Our work has therefore sought to uncover the model of a winning process, not to describe a series of successful management techniques.

Study Findings: A Résumé

Starting from three in-depth case studies and expanding our research net to take in a further nineteen globalization histories, we have proceeded by the method of induction, seeking to establish commonalities across these twenty-two cases. In other words, even though every company's tale of globalization must be considered uniquely influenced by its own context and history, we have sought, and have found, common traits and process characteristics that apply to all the cases. Here is a brief review of our principal findings about globalization's meaning and its business implications:

1. Globalization is a form of expansion distinct from internationalization and multinationalization. A globalizing company creates value for customers by making its offerings (products, services, or competences) available consistently anywhere and anytime. In effect the company learns to compress time and space, giving it what we speak of as a *compressive advantage* from globalization. Globalization's specificity lies in the fact that it gives rise to this new form of advantage—over and above the comparative and competitive advantages already well known in international business.

2. The question of whether to globalize or not arises in an economic environment that obliges the company to ask whether it must find a new form of advantage to survive. If all else is equal in the marketplace, the company may be facing a zero growth future. If rivals or partner companies are already exploiting the compressive advantage, the company may be facing the prospects of losing significant business. Thus the globalization process starts with an analysis of the risks confronting the company.

3. We have distinguished two main categories of risk: the risks arising from not globalizing—elimination and exclusion—and the risks arising from globalizing—imitation and unsustainability. Globalization is never a foregone conclusion; the decision to globalize must be based on a careful weighing of what the company actually faces in terms of risks that make globalization urgent and risks that make globalization difficult to complete.

The basis for the leap to globalization, then, is an analysis concluding that future growth is not possible unless the company redefines its core business to exploit compressive advantage. The risks involved in globalizing imply that the pursuit of compressive advantage is characterized both by urgency and difficulty.

The systematic study of a highly diverse sample of research cases revealed a composite framework of the entrepreneurial process that defines a successful leap to globalization. We stress, however, that no single company in our sample explicitly followed the framework we propose; the framework is our abstraction of the commonalities observed across cases. Three interdependent components appear critical to the management of the globalizing process:

1. *Projection toward globalization*. The globalizing company acts as if globalization were in place from the outset of the drive for international expansion. Rather than gradually building up international experience, as suggested by conventional wisdom, the globalizer appears to take globalization for granted and expands with the objective of exploiting compressive advantage. Projection differs fundamentally from *vision*; successful globalizers do not just predict the future, they act as if what others call the future is in fact the present. For many of the companies studied (for example, Fresenius in medical care and Ispat in steel), the current context does not correspond at all to the entrepreneur's expected state of the world.

2. *Absorption of the economic risks of globalization*. Instead of trying to avoid the risks of globalization, the successful globalizer builds top-notch opportunity capture, global strategy articulation, business practice implementation, and growth management competences and uses these competences to systematically turn risks into opportunities. Thus we have observed the globalizing company to operate in full consciousness of the risks involved in the process: for example, anticipating the needs of partners in order to forestall exclusion and speeding up expansion in order to outrun imitation. This ability to absorb risk permits the company to globalize at great speed.

3. *Harmonization in the face of changing risk intensities*. The decision-making processes of the company ensure that globalizing competences and economic risks stay in tune over time. Harmonization is accomplished by making advance investments in the competences required to confront altered risk constellations in the future and by giving hierarchical priority to actions that respond to the most pressing current risks. Decision-making processes follow a countercyclical pattern and, above all, aim to build a shared understanding of globalization that allows managers in the field to see the broader evolution within which their contributions are embedded.

A Model of the Globalizing Process

We observed projection, absorption, and harmonization in the growth history of every company that made the leap to globalization. Thus it appears that these three management imperatives together represent the hard core of the globalizing process. Nonetheless, before proceeding any further, we would like to warn of erroneous conclusions that might be drawn from our analysis.

As noted earlier, the globalizing process is entrepreneurial and therefore in some degree unique to each firm. This implies that any model of the process should not be applied as a recipe, where one size must fit all. History and context are important to the process, and the components we have highlighted do not come into play with equal force in all companies. Projection, absorption, and harmonization, as well as their subconstructs, are more or less pronounced depending on the needs of the company. A value creation model that focuses on replication, like the model of steel plant turnaround specialist Ispat or coffee marketing innovator Starbucks, will necessarily put more emphasis on business practice implementation than a value creation model that focuses on technology enhancement, like that of Gemplus. Furthermore, projection, absorption, and harmonization are likely to call forth different concrete actions in different contexts: opportunity capture at Fresenius is primarily concerned with acquisitions; at CMS Energy, opportunity capture means the development of new business. Our model of the process provides the necessary *framework* for a leap to globalization—it is not sufficient in itself but needs to be adapted to the specific situation of the globalizing company.

What we can say with confidence from our research data is that successful globalizers develop the entire process we have described, albeit with different accents and emphases. These companies do not "forget" one part of the process, because they are temporarily preoccupied with another. They avoid underestimating any of the key components of the framework. Clearly, entrepreneurial processes do not obey simple, infallible rules; if they did, they would not be entrepreneurial. However, globalization failures do stem from observable, systematic errors. The framework we propose should serve as a reference to ensure that all the critical questions have been asked and addressed. In other words, our research shows how to avoid failure in globalization, not how to guarantee success.

It is also important to recall that what we have described sequentially is in fact a comprehensive process of parallel developments. Projection, absorption, and harmonization are interlinked and mutually enriching. Thus projection and harmonization obey the same logic: by acting as if the future of globalization were already in place, the entrepreneurs leading the globalizing process identify not only the competences required for current success but also those necessary for pushing the next phase. Projection toward globalization and countercyclically jumping the gun on key competence development are closely related in terms of leadership and decision-making process. Similarly, absorption—using the risks of globalization to boost the process of globalizing—is tied to projection and to harmonization.

The several components of the framework are inextricably linked, logically and temporally. Figure 6.1 summarizes the relationships discussed and illustrates the integrity of the process.

Figure 6.1 is our road map; within this road map there is room for every company to prepare and carry out its own leap to globalization, both in accordance with the needs of its own context and in recognition of the indispensable conditions of a successful process.

Management Practices

The study of case histories from sixteen industries, of companies as different from each other as Bombardier and Deutsche Telekom, has also helped us identify the key management practices associated with the leap to globalization. A focus on identifying the concrete measures that recur over the course of the globalizing process

Figure 6.1. The Process of Globalizing: A Road Map.

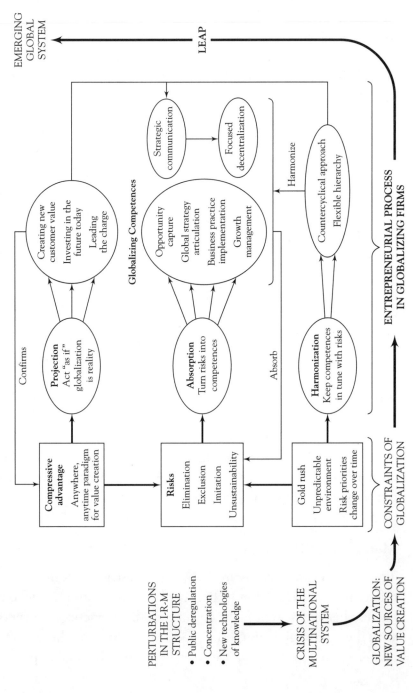

reveals the means through which companies actually manage projection, absorption, and harmonization.

Indeed, cutting through the data presented in the previous chapters, we find that certain management practices come up again and again, in every component of an effective globalizing process. Three management practices appear critical:

1. Globalizing companies are led by individuals who personify the entrepreneurial process.
2. The globalization process involves a continuous flow of communications about strategy.
3. The decisions taken to support globalization often go against received wisdom.

As the preceding chapters have illustrated, each of these three practices plays a central role in implementing projection, absorption, and harmonization.

Considered independently from the process of globalizing, a list of the practices of entrepreneurial leadership, continuous flow of strategy communications, and decisions counter to received wisdom may sound like just another revisiting of well-known management jargon. Indeed, the three management practices described are essential to any strategic change process. What makes it important to examine them in the context of globalization is the timing and the dosage of their use in that process. In other words, as Table 6.1 shows, the key to unlocking the globalization analysis lies in the intersection of process and practice, where framework meets action.

Entrepreneurial leadership does not have the same implications across the practices of projection, absorption, and harmonization. In the first case, projection, the leader's role consists of playing Mr. or Ms. Global, the person who stands tall in representing the new strategy throughout the company (see Chapter Three). In the second case, absorption, not just one leader but a group of leaders has

Table 6.1. Key Management Practices and the Globalizing Process.

Management Practice	Globalizing Process		
	Projection	Absorption	Harmonization
Entrepreneurial leadership	Leads the charge	Articulates global strategy	Communicates the urgency of change
Flow of strategy communications	Creating the basis for new value	Providing support for decentralization	Explaining priority shifts
Decisions counter to received wisdom	Overinvestment	Risks as opportunities	Countercyclical approach

to speak to the external world about the company's global strategy with one voice (see Chapter Four). In the third case, harmonization, the entrepreneurial leader works to convince people in the company of the need to adjust the pecking order of the globalizing competences and stands ready to take the necessary steps to impose a flexible hierarchy (see Chapter Five). In sum, we are not discussing some amorphous need for undefined leadership but the specific kind of entrepreneurial leadership provided by the likes of Gerd Krick at Fresenius and Marc Lassus at Gemplus. Such entrepreneurial leadership is a timely and indispensable ingredient in guiding the globalization process.

In the same way, the continuous flow of strategy communications takes on different meanings with each component of the globalization process. In relation to projection and the attendant reorientation of the core business, the continuous flow of strategy communications shows the different actors in the globalizing company *what* they need to do to create new value and exploit compressive advantage. In relation to absorption and the attendant spread of responsibility, the flow of strategy communications allows decentralized actors to understand *how* they can each contribute to the globalizing process. Finally, in relation to harmonization and the flexible hierarchy it implies, the continuous flow of strategy communications is intended to inform managers *why* the company must adjust the relative positions of competences over time and thus persuade them to accept these changes. In the globalizing process the flow of strategy communications amounts to a lot more than building a shared vision. Again, we see a management commonplace proving its worth in conjunction with timely and targeted application.

Decisions counter to received wisdom also draw their force from situational application. Overinvesting at the outset, treating process risks as opportunities, and taking a countercyclical approach to competence development all contribute to differentiating the globalizing company from rivals facing similar sets of circumstances. Recall that the basis for the leap to globalization is an analysis concluding that future growth is not possible without a redefinition of the core business. Once executives have committed to engaging in the uphill battle of globalization, they cannot win by continuing with business as usual. In this context, the management practice of making decisions counter to received wisdom at every turn in the globalizing process takes on a special meaning as an antidote to inertia and routine.

Sources of Failure

An entrepreneurial process like the leap to globalization can never be fully specified in an abstract model. Seeking such a perfect model would be the management equivalent of the search for the Holy Grail. The best we can do is to construct a model that describes the necessary conditions for success, basing that model on disciplined observation of both successes and failures and inductive reasoning. From this model we can also subsequently deduce the sources of failure or of major difficulty in the process. We found the sources of failure in the globalizing process at three levels: in making the decision to globalize or not, in achieving coherence among the different components of the globalizing process, and in mastering the key management practices.

Making the Decision to Globalize or Not. Because executives' perception of the four globalization risks determines the outcome of the globalization decision (Chapter Two), the quality of that decision is directly related to the ability to accurately gauge those risks. Gauging the risks of elimination, exclusion, imitation, and unsustainability might appear to be the easiest aspect of the globalizing process, but it entails considerable research and thorough deliberation. It is our hope that the tests and attitude map we proposed in Chapter Two will help executives clarify their choices.

Achieving Coherence Among Globalizing Process Components. Here and in the previous chapters, we have pointed out how a lack of coherence among the different components of the globalizing process may result in failure. Projection, absorption, and harmonization need to be managed as a coherent whole. Table 6.2 summarizes the feasibility of globalization in the absence of one or more of the three key process components.

Scenarios A and H are at opposite extremes, characterized by the total presence or total absence of the three principal components of the globalizing process. Scenarios B, C, and D represent an incomplete process in which one of the three components is poorly realized. Under Scenario B, where projection is absent, the company lacks an action pattern that would show stakeholders a clear

Table 6.2. Process Coherence and Globalization Feasibility.

Process Component	Appropriate Use Over the Course of the Process							
Projection	Yes	No	Yes	Yes	Yes	No	No	No
Absorption	Yes	Yes	No	Yes	No	Yes	No	No
Harmonization	Yes	Yes	Yes	No	No	No	Yes	No
Scenario	A	B	C	D	E	F	G	H
Feasibility of Globalization	Maximum		Uncertain			Very difficult		Zero

strategy for globalization. The evolution of strategy may look chaotic, pushed by external events rather than purposefully chosen. Under Scenario C, the company has insufficient competences to absorb risk and may not be able to complete the leap for lack of resources. Under Scenario D, the company fails to adjust its priorities in globalizing competences to changing risk intensities, and a process that might have started out looking promising may fail to survive emerging competitive threats. Scenarios B, C, and D each suffer from a systemic incoherence that jeopardizes the ultimate achievement of globalization.

Under Scenarios E, F, and G, the company appears to be making the leap to globalization only when viewed from a certain angle. The overall process we have described is not in fact at work. Scenario E represents the case in which the company takes significant action toward globalization but fails to build competences and a dynamic of adaptation to changing risks. Globalization is implemented only at the corporate level. Scenario F connotes the existence of globalizing competences in a strategic and procedural vacuum; globalization efforts are likely to be sporadic and isolated. Scenario G implies a sophisticated ability to sense and adjust to changing risks over time, but an absence of strategic clarity and resources. The company has a dynamic of adaptation in place but no clear perspectives.

Even though these scenarios are somewhat artificial in their simplicity, they reveal the logic within the globalizing process. Each of the process components—projection, absorption, and harmonization—contributes in its own way to a complete process, and the absence of one or more of these components puts the process at risk.

Mastering Key Management Practices. The process component scenarios do not speak directly to the question of management practices: if the leap is not to end in failure, decision and process have to be supported throughout by adequate management practices. By asking how the presence or absence of key management practices plays out over the life of the process, we get a more complete picture of the sources of failure in globalizing. Table 6.3 summarizes the different possibilities.

**Table 6.3. Key Management Practices
and Globalization Feasibility.**

Management Practice	Persistence Over the Course of the Process							
Entrepreneurial leadership	Yes	No	Yes	Yes	Yes	No	No	No
Flow of strategy communications	Yes	Yes	No	Yes	No	Yes	No	No
Decisions counter to received wisdom	Yes	Yes	Yes	No	No	No	Yes	No
Scenario	A	B	C	D	E	F	G	H
Feasibility of Globalization	*Maximum*		*Uncertain*			*Very difficult*		*Zero*

Here again, Scenarios A and H are at opposite extremes. Under Scenario A, the three key management practices are observed. If the strategic choice to globalize is correct and the process is managed in a coherent way, then A is the scenario with the *maximum* probability of success. At the opposite extreme, under Scenario H, none of the key management practices is observed, and the probability of making a successful leap to globalization, is in our view, close to zero.

Scenarios B, C, and D each combine two of the three key management practices. Here, the success of the leap to globalization is uncertain. In Scenario B, in which management pushes globalization in the absence of clear leadership over the different components of the process, the company runs the risk of getting stymied when unexpected difficulties appear and no one stands up to maintain the course. Scenario C connotes insufficient flow of strategic communications; this engenders confusion. The globalizing process is endangered because the frontline managers responsible for carrying out decisions are likely to lack understanding of the strategy. Scenario D, in which decisions counter to received wisdom are scarce, implies the presence of internal resistance and the dominance of routine and connotes the danger of slowing down halfway through the leap.

In Scenarios E, F, and G, the company relies on only one of the three key management practices identified in our research. Here the leap to globalization is very difficult. In Scenario E, the company relies on an isolated leader to carry the process, which often does not go beyond speeches and good intentions. Scenario F represents the situation in which strategic planners have put a great deal of work into developing and communicating information on globalization but have not been able to convince the leadership of the company or to initiate concrete actions that would support their analysis. Under this scenario, the globalizing process stays with the planners. Finally, Scenario G illustrates a situation in which entrepreneurial momentum in the company leads to bold decisions counter to received wisdom but lack of information sharing about strategy and insufficient support from the top lead to inconsistency. Here the globalizing process is destined to peter out.

Our analysis of the various subcases involving the globalization decision, process coherence, and management practices is clearly not exhaustive. Nonetheless a careful reading of the tests presented in Chapter Two and of Tables 6.2 and 6.3 can help management identify the majority of difficulties facing the company making a leap to globalization. The point we emphasize here is that the globalizing process itself can be a principal source of failure, over and above the competitive environment. Our hope is that the road maps and scenarios drawn up in this chapter will serve as practical guides to executives contemplating a leap to globalization.

Conclusion

Globalization is not an end in itself. The leap takes the company into new territory but does not fully prepare it for sustaining a competitive advantage. What does managing *after the leap* look like, and how does the company go forward beyond globalization? Our concluding chapter looks into the future of the firm that leaps to globalization.

Conclusion

The Future of the New Globalizers

In this book we have drawn on rich field research data to develop a framework for addressing a new challenge in management—the leap to globalization. Along with our central focus and commentary on the process of globalizing, we have made extensive observations on strategy and structure. Our findings emphasize the entrepreneurial nature of the leap to globalization, suggesting that globalizing is best understood as an entrepreneurial process through which companies dynamically exploit the unique opportunity presented by a changing politico-industrial landscape. Our primary finding is that the leap to globalization is not an act of incremental adaptation but a major transformation with distinct managerial consequences.

Little in the entrepreneurial process framework we have presented is specific to the traditional domain of international management. This does not imply that the variables of concern to international management scholars have disappeared from the picture. Clearly, cultural, political, legal, and practical differences across countries continue to exist. However, and this was an important finding for us, these differences do not appear to be central to the management of the leap to globalization.

Why do national differences play such a minor role? The leap to globalization revolves around managing to meet the needs of the global or globalizing customer. Unlike multinational corporations of old, the new globalizers, although they often have a substantial presence in multiple countries, do not target local sources of customer value, such as preferential access or freedom from trade barriers.

Pursuing compressive advantage, globalizers enter precisely those market segments where national differences can be most readily overcome by an anywhere, anytime offering.

The empirical evidence bears out the importance of the entre-preneurial insight to pursue compressive advantage. If national differences were central to value creation in renal care, for example, it is hardly conceivable that Fresenius could have established a significant market presence in an average of six new countries per year every year since 1995. Again, globalizers do have to deal with national differences, but the very nature of their business models makes national differences less salient than they are for traditional multinationals. Our research shows that once a need for globalization has been diagnosed and a globalization strategy adopted, success has more to do with entrepreneurial processes than with international management skills.

Entrepreneurial Process and Organizational Structure: A Dilemma

Throughout we have emphasized the importance of the *process* of globalizing. Moreover, our data show that the management of globalizing can coexist with the organizational structures already in place. Now we need to ask if the globalizers we studied shift their attention from process to structure as they near the end of their leap. In other words, is the globalizing process a temporary set of actions, competences, and adaptation mechanisms, and is it replaced by a more stable organizational arrangement once the company is well established in a new value creation space? If so, what do globalizers look like in maturity? We can predict that, in theory, stability in a new, global I-R-M configuration will be accompanied by formal restructuring. However, continued instability in institutions, resources, and markets places a premium on entrepreneurship and the kind of entrepreneurial process we have described here. Thus, as Figure 7.1 illustrates, two broad paths of evolution are imaginable.

Figure 7.1. The Future of the New Globalizers: Two Paths of Evolution.

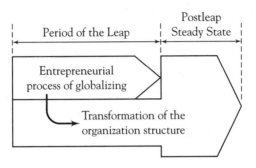

A. Globalizing Process as a Stepping-Stone
to a Global Organization Structure

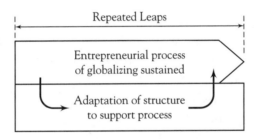

B. Globalizing Process as a Management
Approach for Repeated Leaps

On the first evolutionary path (part A of Figure 7.1), the entrepreneurial process of globalizing occupies but a short, clearly defined moment in time: it is the leap to globalization itself. Once the leap is completed, the process burns out, and the company as a whole adopts a new structure. If this is what happens, it will be interesting to find out what the new global firm resembles. It may resemble the model transnational structure of the 1990s that found its clearest expression in the ABB of CEO Percy Barnevik [1988–1997]). Alternatively, the new structure of globalizing companies may take some novel form.

In the second case (part B of Figure 7.1), the entrepreneurial process of globalizing does not stop with a one-time leap to globalization, but continues to be a viable means of addressing the challenge of repeated leaps. In other words, a company active in several domains may make more than one leap to globalization, with each leap requiring its own entrepreneurial process. In this case the structure of the organization would adapt somewhat to support the specific entrepreneurial process under way but would not fundamentally alter or reach a steady state.

Some Evidence from Our Research

The leap to globalization is still a fresh topic. Neither academic inquiry nor management practice has progressed to the point of proving that one of the two evolutionary paths is more common than the other. Thus the best we can do here is to extrapolate from our experience and from the developing story lines of the companies in our research sample.

As we have noted, a striking feature of successful globalizers is that the entrepreneurs who have led the most spectacular leaps (people like Marc Lassus, Bernie Ebbers, and Gerd Krick) never gave management priority to organizational structure or global organization as such. Above all, these leaders wanted the organization to be adaptable, so that the managers involved in the leap would be able do their jobs in the face of rapidly changing circumstances. For example, at Fresenius the *Unternehmer* structure of self-managing units enables distributed decision making, but the *Unternehmen* are not the focus of the globalizing process. Conversely, a number of companies that have had difficulty launching their leaps to globalization—BT, for example—appeared to view the challenge of globalizing primarily in structural terms and moved to put a complex global organization in place before taking decisive action on customer value. This observation suggests that a focus on structure over process is generally not compatible with embarking on leap growth. Rushing to reach a steady state and capping the leap to globalization with a global structure may therefore preclude acting on further opportunities to leap.

Perhaps the most pertinent observation we can make at the time this book goes to press is that the majority of the twenty-two companies in our research sample are still (or again) in a state of transition. Thus Gemplus's preoccupation is with navigating the move from products to solutions, as the basis of advantage in smart cards shifts from card makers to software writers and solutions providers. Similarly, Check Point is working through a product changeover, going from offering firewall software to offering virtual private network solutions; Fresenius is focusing on building global leadership in its business lines other than renal care. It is remarkable that none of these companies is giving primary attention to organizational structure: indeed, a global structure like ABB's, with intersecting product, region, and country reporting lines, is rarely even talked about in these circles, let alone seriously considered for implementation.

Of course none of the companies we studied has reached the size or state of complexity of a long-established multinational like ABB or Citibank. Perhaps the companies in our research sample have simply not completed their leap and are still in the process of organizing their new multicountry presence. Interestingly, the current globalization efforts of companies like Gemplus and Fresenius are not limited to carrying the same set of activities as before into new countries. Rather these companies seem to be extending the exploitation of compressive advantage to other, related domains of business. A remark Gerd Krick made several years ago to Matthias Schmidt, the head of Fresenius's Pharma division, comes to mind: "we did it [achieved global leadership] in Dialysis . . . we have to do the same thing in Pharma."

Repeated Leaps and the Extension of Globalization

If future developments bear out the latter set of ideas, our thinking about the process of globalization will require revision. Rather than describing globalization as a single leap, we would need to consider globalization as *a series of leaps*, each one of which allows a company to enlarge its domain of compressive advantage exploitation. It is important at this point to distinguish the process of performing repeated leaps to globalization from the process of taking multiple products across countries. The multinational with multiple product lines builds on its superior ability to coordinate activities across countries, to diversify, whereas the *serial globalizer* seeks to exploit compressive advantage across multiple domains (as depicted in Figure 7.2).

Why would globalizers seek to engage in repeated leaps? On the one hand, and consistent with classic arguments in strategy if not in finance, domain expansion reduces portfolio risk. Being active in several domains buffers the company against poor conditions in any one of those domains. On the other hand, perhaps more pressing to globalizers and more economically sound than the portfolio risk argument, is the need to cope with the high risk of imitation in globalization. As we have seen in companies as diverse as WorldCom and Ispat, the exploitation of compressive advantage quickly draws imitators and is very hard to sustain. To avoid imitation, then, globalizers would seek to engage in repeated leaps, always trying to leap before others.

Figure 7.2. Repeated Leaps to Globalization.

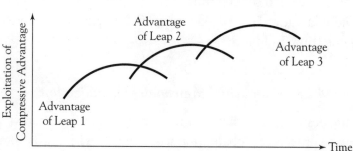

Indeed, successful globalizers may be better able than rivals to engage in repeated leaps, because they have mastered the process of globalizing. In contrast to their counterparts at established multinationals, who have developed the optimization of multinational efficiency to a fine art, the managers of the new globalizers know how to take a business from one state of the world to another. The company that can manage the process we have described in this book might (1) move into related businesses that are on the threshold of globalizing, (2) acquire or merge with other firms in need of globalizing skills, or (3) help alliance partners to globalize.

Bombardier, for example, has globalized both in aircraft and in train cars in temporally overlapping leaps. Over the last ten years the company has established value-added operations in more than twenty countries and sales in more than forty. This pattern of growth could be explained in a traditional manner by saying that the company engaged in related diversification on the basis of superior manufacturing. One could also say, however, that the company has developed know-how in manufacturing management, planning, and negotiation that when coupled with an ability to run the globalizing process allows the company to extend the exploitation of compressive advantage to multiple domains. In fact the company is not stopping at aircraft and train cars but is currently actively pursuing new initiatives to globalize in electronic vehicles and capital investment financing.

Bombardier is a serial globalizer. The company-specific know-how and globalizing process skill of its first leaps to globalization continue to be redeployed in new domains. Remarkably, the company has maintained essentially the same structure since 1985, a structure put in place to deal with diversification, not globalization. Indeed, to maintain the entrepreneurial spirit that has characterized the company's growth thus far, Bombardier management explicitly shies away from putting a more complicated, explicitly global structure in place. With reference to the elaborate cross-subsidiary knowledge-sharing procedures implied in a global structure, Executive Vice President Yvan Allaire once said, "We do not want to become a learning bureaucracy." At Bombardier the entre-preneurial process of globalizing appears to coexist with a more tra-ditional, nonglobal organizational structure.

If our observations of the current situations at Bombardier, Gemplus, WorldCom, and others are borne out over time, our def-inition of what constitutes globalization will have to be expanded. Globalization may come to be seen as a process of multiplying leaps in order to build a global portfolio of compressive advantage. In that case the path of evolution traced on part B of Figure 7.1 will be shown to be closest to the reality of globalizers: the successful glob-alizer would engage in repeated leaps, continuing to maintain both a rather simple organizational structure that is not efficiency maxi-mizing in steady state and a powerful entrepreneurial process to sup-port leap growth. The art of managing this globalizing company would center on maintaining a balance between structure and process rather than on searching for an ideal organization that brings a global structure and the globalizing process under one hat.

Further Research

The previous discussion of the future of the new globalizers illus-trates the kinds of hypotheses and research directions that are emerging from the work presented in this book. The globalization process is too recent for us to establish certainties. To complete the work begun here, it will be necessary to learn more about the process and to follow up on the developing stories of the companies pursuing globalization. A first task will be to seek corroboration for our findings in a larger sample of companies. If the leap to global-ization is indeed a general phenomenon in today's economy, it will be particularly important to identify and map the sources of com-pressive advantage as they are exploited by different companies, in-dustry by industry.

A second direction for further research will be to explore in greater detail the hypothesis that globalizing companies tend to make repeated leaps. It may be especially rewarding to study how the relationship between entrepreneurial process and organizational structure plays out when a company has the increased scope of compressive advantage exploitation that many globalizers are now reaching for. Will it be necessary or possible to stop the leaping process to stabilize the organization? The economic conditions that make repeated leaps desirable and the managerial adjustments that make repeated leaps feasible are also important areas for further study.

A third research direction that can be derived from the research we have reported here is an exploration of the ways established multinational firms move to exploit compressive advantage. Today, classic multinationals like ABB, Alcatel, and Siemens strongly emphasize *entrepreneurial spirit* and *entrepreneurial action*. Is there a link between the need for entrepreneurship in these companies and the forces for globalization described here? Are not many of the model multinationals of old in fact trying to make the leap to globalization in selected businesses? If so, they may be able to learn something about the required entrepreneurial process from companies that are smaller and less well established but perfectly focused on globalization. In any case the particular challenges inherent in multinationals' size and past (and the need for an entrepreneurial "propensity for action" as a prerequisite for leaping, as discussed in Chapter Two) is likely to make the study of any multinational's quest to exploit compressive advantage very interesting.

This book is a work of observation and analysis. Although we cannot treat a subject as new and as rich as the leap to globalization comprehensively at this time, our research has nonetheless led us to several important findings and suggested a number of intriguing propositions. The leap to globalization is an entrepreneurial process. Our framework explains the logic and describes the workings of this process. As researchers and consultants, our goal has been to contribute to building knowledge about complex phenomena, motivating scholars with ideas for further study, and providing executives with tools for action.

Appendix:
Research Methods

The findings reported in this book are based on four years of field-based research into the process of globalizing. As noted in the Introduction, this process has not been previously explored by academics or other researchers. Moreover, it poses significant questions for existing research on the multinational company and the internationalization process. The lack of prior research on the topic and these new questions implied that extant theoretical bases offered inadequate support for our inquiry. We therefore chose an inductive research approach, studying a small sample of companies in detail, with the objective of surfacing common patterns in the way globalizing is managed. In order to reduce the effects of size, industry, and country bias in our findings and reveal the underlying patterns of successful globalization, we made an effort to ensure maximum variety in the sample of companies studied. The inquiry covered twenty-two companies from sixteen industrial sectors and nine home countries. The companies varied in size from start-ups with revenues in the millions to giants with annual sales in the double-digit billions. All the companies in our sample had declared globalization to be a prime objective and had undertaken significant efforts to globalize in a short time. Some have done very well, coming out on top of their industry races and providing shareholders with superior returns; others have had to accept costly setbacks. In some cases the globalization game is still playing out, and success and failure are not yet clearly distinguishable.

Conducted according to the tenets of grounded theory building, the research proceeded in two phases. In the first phase, we
conducted in-depth case studies of the globalization histories of
three companies from very different contexts: smart card pioneer
Gemplus, a French start-up in a new industry; CMS Energy, a domestic U.S. utility in a deregulating industry; and renal care specialist Fresenius, a multinational German company in a nationally
fragmented industry. These case studies drew on publicly available
data, company archives, and multiple, extensive interviews with
both senior executives and managers of operations in the field. On
average we conducted over thirty hours of interviews per company,
close to one hundred hours altogether (see Table A.1).

The majority of interviews were both tape-recorded and manu-
ally transcribed. During all of the interviews at Gemplus and about
half the interviews at CMS Energy, the authors were assisted by research assistants. The interview questions were aimed at building a
chronology of events and took a "when did you do what" form. At
no time did we suggest causal links to the interviewees; if the interviewees offered causal explanations, these were noted and, where
possible, verified against company documents. We have maintained
a research relationship with each of the three companies and periodically revisit to gather more data and update our information base.

In this first phase of the study, we carefully reconstructed the individual globalization histories of the three companies. We then
compared the histories to identify any behaviors or processes common to the three companies. The following elements could be observed—in various shapes and forms—across the companies:

- *The important role of a key leader within a broader process.* In
  each of the three companies, one executive clearly led the
  globalization effort, but every one of these executives stressed
  the importance of putting a process in place that got many
  people in the organization involved.

- *A determination to turn risks into opportunities.* The behaviors and
  management actions of the companies studied demonstrated

Table A.1. Interviews at CMS Energy, Fresenius, and Gemplus.

	CMS Energy	Fresenius	Gemplus
Primary interview partners	William McCormick, CEO Vic Fryling, COO Al Wright, CFO Rodney Boulanger, CEO, independent power production Laura Mountcastle, vice president, investor relations Joseph Tomasik, director of development, EMEA (Europe, Middle East, Africa) Francisco Mezzadri, general manager, Latin America John McGloughlin, director of development, Latin America Enrique Wolff, director, Entre Rios Corlos Principi, director of operations, Latin America Also, plant managers, business developers, and management staff	Dr. Gerd Krick, CEO Dr. Matthias Schmidt, director, Pharma Dr. Werner Brandt, CFO, Fresenius Medical Care Friedrich Werner, director, human resources Edward Jamieson, president, Canada Christian Fischer, controller Also, plant managers, business developers, and management staff	Marc Lassus, chairman Daniel LeGal, CEO Pat Jones, CFO Jacques Seneca, executive vice president, development Pascal Didier, vice president, strategy Thian Yee Chua, managing director, Japan Michael Crosno, executive vice president, North America Also, plant managers, business developers, and management staff
Interview locations	Dearborn, Michigan London Buenos Aires	Bad Homburg, Germany Paris	Gémenos, France London Redwood City, California
Time	1997–2001	1997–2001	1997–2001

a clear recognition of both the risks of action and the risks of inaction in the context of globalization. Globalization did not present itself as a blind adventure but as a series of well-calculated steps for dealing with competitive threats.

- *An emphasis not on new structure but on people, timing, and context in an entrepreneurial growth process.* Not one of the three companies conceived of globalization in terms of a search for a new, ideal organizational structure.

On the basis of these common elements and a detailed comparison of the companies' time lines of key events, we sketched the outlines of a management framework, a first attempt to reconcile objective case data, the personal accounts of the companies' executives, and academic perspectives familiar to us from our professional activities as researchers and teachers. Although the academic literature on the globalizing *process* itself is scant, the literature on topics related to globalization and the management of global business enterprises is vast and highly segmented. Our research work drew heavily on this literature, and the Bibliography at the end of this book lists the intellectual roots against which we tested our emerging ideas.

The preliminary conclusions drawn from the three first-phase case studies were tested and further refined in a larger but necessarily less detailed follow-up study of nineteen companies that had also embarked upon the leap to globalization and established a presence in dozens of countries in a very short time.

Companies Studied in the Second Phase, by Industry

Telecommunications: British Telecommunications (BT), Deutsche Telekom, Telefonica, WorldCom

Utilities: Enron, National Power, Thames Water

Transport: Bombardier

Cement: Cemex

Steel: Ispat

Dairy: Parmalat

Restaurant: Starbucks

Retail: Wal-Mart

Information services: Bloomberg

Internet: Check Point, DoubleClick

Software: Infosys

Engineering: Fluor

Banking: Banco Santander (now BSCH)

As in the first phase, we sought maximum variety in our sample. The objective of this second phase was to deepen our understanding of the actions and behaviors associated with the leap to globalization and to test for exceptions to the patterns developed in the first phase. For each of these nineteen companies, we oversaw the writing of globalization cases based on publicly available data and, for fifteen out of the nineteen companies, personal interviews that we and our students conducted with company executives (spending two to ten hours per company interviewing one to six executives). At the four companies where personal interviews were not possible, we relied on material from associate researchers who had conducted interviews at the companies in question.

The second phase of the study was particularly helpful in clarifying the following points:

- The nature of the core business transformation implied by globalization.
- The types of globalizing competences and their contextually modified applications.
- The relationship between the globalizing process and the evolution of organizational structure.

This two-phase research design allowed us to work out the commonalities and the differences among the companies studied. From the mass of data at our disposal, we induced the patterns of successful and unsuccessful globalizing processes. Interestingly and more than a little surprisingly, we found that companies from very different contexts shared a great deal. By working through the economic logic and processual coherence of the recurring patterns observed and drawing on a careful reading of the globalization and entrepreneurial process literatures, we began to develop a synthesis that described the management of the globalizing process.

We completed our work by articulating a framework that is intentionally formal. This step takes our discussion beyond a collection of stories and creates a representation that can be of use in the study of other companies facing the same set of issues. Having eliminated the idiosyncrasies of the three initial case study companies from our modeling of the leap to globalization by virtue of the second-phase test, we built a parsimonious, generic framework that incorporated the principal findings of the study. This framework has an internal logic that allows the reader to see how actions and reactions that might appear unrelated form a coherent whole.

This book is a summary of our research. As our choice of methodologies indicates, our framework does not portray the individual realities of all the companies studied nor does its use guarantee success. The framework puts together elements that may appear disparate individually but that can be combined in a coherent and logical way to reveal the dynamics of the leap to globalization. This generic framework should encourage researchers and practitioners to bring their own data and experience to bear on the issues raised here. We hope that further in-depth research will add substantial extensions to the framework.

Bibliography

Amin, S. (1997). *Capitalism in the age of globalization*. London: Zed Books.

Arthur, W. B. (1989). Competing technologies, increasing returns, and lock-in by historical events. *The Economic Journal*, 99, 116–131.

Arthur, W. B. (1994). *Increasing returns and path dependence in the economy*. Ann Arbor: University of Michigan Press.

Atamer T., Calori, R., & Nunès, P. (1999). *The dynamics of international competition*. Thousand Oaks, CA: Sage.

Baden-Fuller, C.W.F., & Stopford, J. M. (1991). Globalization frustrated: The case of white goods. *Strategic Management Journal*, 12, 493–498.

Ballek, B., Kimura, M., & Salloux, S. (1999). *Gemplus*. Case No. 99–000–10. London: London Business School.

Barney, J. (1986). Strategic factor markets: Expectations, luck and business strategy. *Management Science*, 32, 1231–1241.

Barney, J. (1991). Firm resources and sustained competitive advantage. *Journal of Management*, 17, 99–120.

Bartlett, C. A. (1982, Summer). How multinational organizations evolve. *Journal of Business Strategy*, pp. 20–32.

Bartlett, C. A., & Ghoshal, S. (1989). *Managing across borders: The transnational solution*. Boston: Harvard Business School Press.

Bartlett, C. A., & Ghoshal, S. (1991, Summer). Global strategic management: Impact on the new frontiers of strategy research. *Strategic Management Journal*, 12, 5–17.

Benito, G.R.G., & Gripsrud, G. (1992). The expansion of foreign direct investments: Discrete rational location choices or a cultural learning process? *Journal of International Business Studies*, 23, 461–476.

Birkinshaw, J., Morrison, A. J., & Hulland, J. (1995). Structural and competitive determinants of global integration strategy. *Strategic Management Journal*, 16, 637–655.

Blumenthal, W. M. (1988). The world economy and technological change. *Foreign Affairs*, 66, 529–550.

Boyer, R. (1990). *The regulation school: A critical introduction*. New York: Columbia University Press.

Braudel, F. (1992). *The wheels of commerce: Civilization and capitalism: 15th-18th century*. Berkeley: University of California Press.

Brooks, H., & Guile, B. R. (1987). Overview. In B. R. Guile & H. Brooks (Eds.), *Technology and global industry* (pp. 1–15). Washington, DC: National Academy Press.

Casson, M., & Associates. (1986). *Multinationals and world trade*. London: Allen and Unwin.

Caves, R. E., Khalilzadeh-Shirazi, J., & Porter. M. E. (1975). Scale economies in statistical analyses of market power. *Review of Economics and Statistics, 57,* 133–140.

Clark, T., Pugh, D. S., & Mallory, G. (1997). The process of internationalization in the operating firm. *International Business Review, 6,* 605–609.

Commons, J. (1934). *Institutional economics*. Madison: University of Wisconsin Press.

Crook, S., Pakuslki, J., & Waters, M. (1992). *Postmodernization*. Thousand Oaks, CA: Sage.

Dicken, P. (1998). *Global shift: Transforming the world economy* (3rd ed.). London: Chapman.

Dierickx, J., & Cool, K. (1989). Asset stock accumulation and the sustainability of competitive advantage. *Management Science, 35,* 1504–1514.

Dosi, G., & Kogut, B. (1993). National specificities and the context of change: The coevolution of organization and technology. In B. Kogut (Ed.), *Country competitiveness: Technology and the organizing of work* (pp. 249–262). Oxford: Oxford University Press.

Doz, Y. L. (1978, Fall). Manufacturing rationalization within multinational companies. *Columbia Journal of World Business*, pp. 82–94.

Doz, Y. L. (1987). International industries: Fragmentation versus globalization. In B. R. Guile & H. Brooks (Eds.), *Technology and global industry* (pp. 96–118). Washington, DC: National Academy Press.

Doz, Y. L., Bartlett, C. A., & Prahalad, C. K. (1981, Spring). Global competitive pressures and host country demands. *California Management Review*, pp. 63–74.

Dunning, J. H. (1980). Towards an eclectic theory of international production: Some empirical tests. *Journal of International Business Studies, 11,* 9–31.

Egelhoff, W. G. (1988). *Organizing the multinational enterprise: An information processing perspective*. New York: Ballinger.

Eliasson, G. (1990). *The knowledge-based information economy*. Stockholm: Almquist and Wiksell International.

Fayerweather, J. (1969). *International business management: A conceptual framework*. New York: McGraw-Hill.

Foray, D., & Lundvall, B. A. (Eds.). (1996). *Employment and growth in the knowledge-based economy*. Paris: Organization for Economic Cooperation and Development.

Geller, M. (2000, March). Ten minutes with . . . Tim Koogle. *The NASDAQ International Magazine*, pp. 14–18.

Gersick, C.J.G. (1994). Pacing strategic change: The case of a new venture. *Academy of Management Journal, 37*, 9–45.

Ghoshal, S. (1987). Global strategy: An organizing framework. *Strategic Management Journal, 8*, 425–440.

Giddens, A. (1990). *The consequence of modernity*. Cambridge, UK: Polity Press.

Gordon, D. (1980). Stage of accumulation and long economic cycles. In T. Hopkins & I. Wallerstein (Eds.), *Processes of world systems*. Thousand Oaks, CA: Sage.

Gottdiener, M., & Komninos, N. (Eds.). (1989). *Capitalist development and crisis theory: Accumulation, regulation and spatial restructuring*. London: St. Martin's Press.

Greenfield, D. (2001, July). Security council. *The NASDAQ International Magazine*, pp. 52–55.

Guehenno, J.-M. (1995). *The end of the nation-state*. St. Paul: University of Minnesota Press.

Hamel, G., & Prahalad, C. K. (1985, July–August). Do you really have a global strategy? *Harvard Business Review*, pp. 139–148.

Harvey, D. (1989). *The condition of postmodernity*. Oxford: Blackwell.

Hay, G. A., & Werden, G. J. (1993). Horizontal mergers: Law, policy, and economics. *American Economic Review, 83*, 173–178.

Heenan, D. A., & Perlmutter, H. V. (1979). *Multinational organization development*. Reading, MA: Addison-Wesley.

Hennart, J.-F. (1982). *A theory of the multinational corporation*. Ann Arbor: University of Michigan Press.

Hirst, P., & Thompson, G. (1992). The problem of "globalization": International economic relations, national economic management and the formation of trading blocs. *Economy and Society, 24*, 408–442.

Hollingsworth, J. R., & Boyer, R. (Eds.). (1997). *Contemporary capitalism: The embeddedness of institutions*. Cambridge, UK: Cambridge University Press.

Holloway, N. (1999, April 19). Bombardier's master builder. *Forbes*, pp. 162–165.

Irwin, D. A. (1996). The United States in a new global economy? A century's perspective. *American Economic Review, 86*, 41–47.

Johanson, J., & Vahlne, J.-E. (1977). The internationalization process of the firm: A model of knowledge development and increasing foreign market commitments. *Journal of International Business Studies, 8*, 23–32.

Johanson, J., & Vahlne, J.-E. (1990). The mechanism of internationalization. *International Marketing Review, 7*, 11–24.

Kindleberger, C. (1969). *American business abroad*. New Haven, CT: Yale University Press.

Kobrin, S. J. (1991). An empirical analysis of the determinants of global integration. *Strategic Management Journal, 12*, 17–31.

Kogut, B. (1994, Fall). Normative observations on the value added chain and strategic groups. *Journal of International Business Studies*, pp. 151–168.

Korine, H. D. (1999a). *Bombardier.* Case no. 99-000-20. London: London Business School.

Korine, H. D. (1999b). *CMS Energy.* Case no. 99-000-17. London: London Business School.

Korine, H. D. (1999c). *Fresenius A.G.: Globalization.* Case no. 99-000-13. London: London Business School.

Levitt, T. (1983, May-June). The globalization of markets. *Harvard Business Review*, pp. 92–102.

Leyshon, A. (1996). Dissolving difference? Money, disembedding and the creation of "global finance space." In P. W. Daniels & W. F. Lever (Eds.), *Global economy in transition* (pp. 62–80). Harlow, UK: Longman.

Lieberman M. B., & Montgomery, D. B. (1988). First mover advantages. *Strategic Management Journal*, 9, 41–58.

Lippman, S., & Rumelt, R. (1982). Uncertain imitability: An analysis of interfirm differences in efficiency under competition. *Bell Journal of Economics*, 13, 418–438.

Lorange, P. (Ed.). (1988). *Cooperative strategies in international business.* San Francisco: New Lexington Press.

Lundvall, B. A., & Johnson, B. (1994). The learning economy. *Journal of Industry Studies*, 1(2), 23–42.

Magee, S. P. (1977). Information and the multinational corporation: An appropriability theory of foreign direct investment. In J. N. Baghwati (Ed.), *The New International Economic Order* (pp. 317–340). Cambridge, MA: MIT Press.

Malnight, T. W. (1995). Globalization of an ethnocentric firm: An evolutionary perspective. *Strategic Management Journal*, 16, 119–142.

Malnight, T. W. (1996). The transition from decentralized to network-based MNC structures: An evolutionary perspective. *Journal of International Business Studies*, 27, 43–65.

Marzloff, B., & Glaziou, S. (1999). *Le temps des puces.* Paris: Carnot.

Mathews, J. A., & Snow, C. C. (1999a). *Accelerated internationalization: The globalization strategies of latecomer firms* (Working paper).

Mathews, J. A., & Snow, C. C. (1999b). *A resource-based view of the firm's international expansion* (Working paper).

McGrew, B. G. (1992). Conceptualizing global politics. In B. G. McGrew and P. G. Lewis (Eds.), *Global politics: Globalization and the nation state.* Cambridge, UK: Polity Press.

McLuhan, M. (1964). *Understanding media.* London: Routledge.

McLuhan, M., & Fiore, Q. (1970). *War and peace in the global village* (2nd ed.). London: Allen Lane.

Melin, L. (1992). Internationalization as a strategy process. *Strategic Management Journal, 13,* 98–118.

Nelson, R. (1998). The co-evolution of technology, industrial structure and supporting institutions. In G. Dosi, D. Teece, & J. Chystry (Eds.), *Technology, organization, and competitiveness* (pp. 319–332). Oxford: Oxford University Press.

North, D. (1990). *Institutions, institutional change and economic performance.* Cambridge, MA: Harvard University Press.

North, D. (1991). Institutions. *Journal of Economic Perspectives, 5,* 97–112.

Ohmae, K. (1995). *End of the nation state: The rise of regional economies.* New York: Free Press.

Ostry, S., & Nelson, R. R. (1995). *Techno-nationalism and techno-globalism: Conflict and cooperation.* Washington, DC: Brookings Institution.

Oviatt, B. M., & McDougall, P. P. (1994). Toward a theory of international new ventures. *Journal of International Business Studies, 25,* 45–64.

Oviatt, B. M., & McDougall, P. P. (1995). Global start-ups: Entrepreneurs on a worldwide stage. *Academy of Management Executive, 9,* 30–43.

Pendergrast, M. (2001, July). Make that to go. *The NASDAQ International Magazine,* pp. 47–51.

Penrose, E. T. (1959). *The theory of the growth of the firm.* Oxford: Blackwell.

Perlmutter, H. V. (1969). The tortuous evolution of the multinational corporation. *Columbia Journal of World Business, 4,* 8–18.

Porter, M. (1986). Competition in global industries: A conceptual framework. In M. Porter (Ed.), *Competition in global industries.* Boston: Harvard Business School Press.

Porter, M. (1990). *The competitive advantage of nations.* New York: Free Press.

Prahalad, C. K., & Doz, Y. (1987). *The multinational mission: Balancing local demands and global vision.* New York: Free Press.

Ricardo, D. (1992). *On the principles of political economy and taxation.* London: Dent. (Original work published 1817)

Roberston, R. (1992). *Globalization.* Thousand Oaks, CA: Sage.

Rumelt, R. P. (1984). Towards a strategic theory of the firm. In R. B. Lamb (Ed.), *Competitive strategic management* (pp. 566–570). Upper Saddle River, NJ: Prentice Hall.

Russo, M. V. (1992). Bureaucracy, economic regulation, and the incentive limits of the firm. *Strategic Management Journal, 13,* 103–129.

Scherer, F. (1980). *Industrial market structure and economic performance.* Skokie, IL: Rand-McNally.

Schmalensee, R. (1978). Entry deterrence and the ready-to-eat breakfast cereal industry. *Bell Journal of Economics, 86,* 305–327.

Schumpeter, J. A. (1939). *Business cycles.* New York: McGraw-Hill.

Schumpeter, J. A. (1942). *Capitalism, socialism and democracy.* New York: McGraw-Hill.

Schumpeter, J. A. (1989). *Essays on entrepreneurs, innovations, business cycles, and the evolution of capitalism.* New Brunswick, NJ: Transaction.

Shapiro, C., & Varian, H. R. (1998). *Information rules: A strategic guide to the network economy.* Cambridge, MA: Harvard Business School Press.

Strange, S., & Stopford, J. M. (1991). *Rival states, rival firms: Competition for world market shares.* Cambridge, UK: Cambridge University Press.

Teece, D. J. (1977, June). Technology transfer by multinational firms: The resource cost of transferring technological know-how. *Economic Journal,* pp. 242–261.

Teece, D. J. (1980). The diffusion of an administrative innovation. *Management Science, 26,* 464–470.

Teece, D. J. (1981, November). The market for know-how and the efficient international transfer of technology. *Annals,* pp. 81–96.

Tirole, J. (1988). *The theory of industrial organization.* Cambridge, MA: MIT Press.

Tushman, M. L., & Romanelli, E. (1985). Organizational evolution: A metamorphosis model of convergence and reorientation. In L. L. Cumming and B. L. Stan (Eds.), *Research in organizational behavior* (Vol. 7, pp. 171–222). Greenwich, CT: JAI Press.

Vernon, R. (1974). The location of economic activity. In J. H. Dunning (Ed.), *Economic analysis and the multinational enterprise* (pp. 89–114). London: Allen and Unwin.

Waters, M. (1995). *Globalization (key ideas).* London: Routledge.

Yip, G. (1992). *Total global strategy.* Upper Saddle River, NJ: Prentice Hall.

Index

The Authors

Harry Korine is assistant professor of strategic and international management at the London Business School. He has published a number of academic articles and case studies in the field of strategic management and acted as consultant to several large companies. His current research focuses on entrepreneurship in strategy and the management of the globalization process.

Pierre-Yves Gomez is professor of strategy and director of the Rodolphe Mérieux Foundation for Entrepreneurial Management at the École de Management de Lyon. His prior books include *Qualité et théorie des conventions* (1994), *Le gouvernement de l'entreprise* (1996), and *La République des Actionnaires* (2001) (all in French). He is also the editor of *Trust, Firms and Society* (1997). His current research focuses on corporate governance and the management of the globalization process.